Praise for *Their Borders, Ou*

"All around the world the cry from the street is 'Free Palestine.' This vital and varied collection reveals some of the global solidarities that lie beneath that united cry, and in doing so asks us to consider what connections we can make, and what histories we might reshape—together."
—Kamila Shamsie

"*Their Borders, Our World* arrives as a meteor, incandescent, a signal of determination and solidarity in a dark time, assuring that Palestine will be free."
—Roxanne Dunbar-Ortiz

"From exploring settler colonialism's banality to the violence of architecture, this timely, highly recommended book explores, through ten innovative essays, new insights into ways of understanding and building solidarities with Palestine."
—Raja Shehadeh

"Edward Said once remarked Palestinians had been denied the permission to narrate their own histories and experiences. Much has changed since then. *Their Borders, Our World* brings together writers from PalFest, the international cultural solidarity initiative that defies the bans, borders, and bigotry aimed at snuffing out the vibrant Palestinian literary tradition. In the shadow of a Western-backed annihilationist campaign against Gaza and Palestinians, this volume does more than grant the permission to narrate: it is, without permission or apology, a call to liberate."
—Nick Estes (Lakota)

THEIR BORDERS, OUR WORLD

Building New Solidarities with Palestine

EDITED BY MAHDI SABBAGH

Published in 2024 by
Haymarket Books
P.O. Box 180165
Chicago, IL 60618
www.haymarketbooks.org

ISBN: 979-8-88890-099-4

Distributed to the trade in the US through Consortium Book Sales and Distribution (www.cbsd.com) and internationally through Ingram Publisher Services International (www.ingramcontent.com).

This book was published with the generous support of Lannan Foundation, Wallace Action Fund, Marguerite Casey Foundation, and the Matakyev Research Fellowship at the Center for Imagination in the Borderlands (Arizona State University).

Special discounts are available for bulk purchases by organizations and institutions. Please email info@haymarketbooks.org for more information.

Cover and interior artwork by Bráulio Amado.
Cover and interior design by Tala Safié.

Library of Congress Cataloging-in-Publication data is available.

10 9 8 7 6 5 4 3 2 1

This volume is dedicated to my grandmother Sumayyah Khoury, who taught me solidarity by example when her family, among many families in Nazareth, hid and housed the people of Saffuriyeh when their village was destroyed by Israeli forces in 1948. Thank you for teaching us how to live together.

CONTENTS

Foreword

February 12, 2024

It is the fifth month of Israel's genocidal assault against Palestinians in Gaza. I know that by the time this book is printed and read by you, it will be worse than it is today. Today, Israel has killed more than 27,000 Palestinians in four months, displaced nearly two million, starved the entire population through the winter, destroyed the healthcare system, and is poised to invade Rafah, the last standing city in Gaza, where most of the population is sheltering.

What is happening is both shocking and a clear continuation of decades of Israeli policy aimed at the total domination and expulsion of Palestinian life. That policy has been enacted on the ground with settlement building, demolition of homes and villages, unlawful arrests, the wall, the checkpoints, the killing and beating of Palestinians throughout the land, and the seventeen-year siege on Gaza. It has also been enacted on the level of discourse and ideas, with Israel's seemingly inexhaustible commitment to control what is sayable and what is not when it comes to Palestine in the Western world in particular. It knows that its material existence as an ethnostate and an occupying military relies on the maintenance of an inverted understanding of power among the populations of the United States and other patron governments. For decades, it has successfully produced and safeguarded a cultural view that Israel is a weak state surrounded by hostile, armed Arabs, that all Palestinian action toward freedom is terrorism, that Israel represents Judaism, that a people who survived a genocide cannot perpetrate another, and that the eruptions of conflict in and around Palestine are about embedded religious feuds, rather than a people struggling against a consistently expansionist racist state structure. Israel has successfully made vocal support of this view a prerequisite for viable presidential candidacy in the US.

Networks of international political and military support for Israel are as essential to Zionism's colonial project today as they were a century ago, and they have proven embedded and intransigent to a level that many did not believe was possible. It is this active complicity that demands that we continue to speak, fight, write, disrupt, boycott, and escalate our tactics wherever we are. It is this that moves us from our despair and paralysis, when it is so clear that all of the images and exposure and witnessing of trembling children and broken bodies and numbered, naked, blindfolded, executed Palestinian men, that all of the op-eds and rallies and speeches and discursive progress and mainstreaming of the Palestinian cause, all of it is too slow, too slow to stop the catastrophe that is happening, too slow to stop the unspeakable pain and suffering. One wants to give up, to say there is no point, that the only action worth doing is to chain one's self to the right fence, to physically stop the movement of weapons. And this, too, we should do. But we learn from Palestinians, as we learn from struggling people throughout history, the irreplaceable value of the long horizon, the crucial role of the idea, of the narration of experience, of the direct questioning of domination, and of the creativity summoned in surviving that

which we are not meant to survive. We learn that Zionism and other fascist nationalist projects operate, psychologically, beyond our biological timelines and depend on our thought being limited by them. They count on our exhaustion, on our despair, our giving up, and so we must discipline and train our minds and our politics to see longer, to look farther: to look alongside those struggling, and not simply at them.

As I write this, Palestinians in Gaza are saying they refuse to leave Rafah, where many of them have now been twice- or thrice-displaced in the last four months, hungry, cold, and under constant attack. They refuse to leave and be killed in ever-less dignified conditions. They refuse to leave and be separated from the family they have been able to survive with. They care for and bury children who are not their own, report through their heartbreak and homelessness. When the bombs stop falling, we will hear more about the horrors that Israel has committed. We will also hear about the difficult and inspiring things people are doing to survive. No one should have to be a hero, and it does not lighten the horror of the crime. But this is what humans do, in their struggle for life. Who am I to give up? Who are we?

Gaza—enterprising and besieged, ancient and crowded, overlooked and at the core—has shattered several lies: that colonialism is in the past, that Israel is special and should be treated as such, and that Palestinians do not exist.

Anti-colonial thinkers from Césaire to Fanon and Kanafani show us how imperial societies make the subjects that they dominate but are also made by them. American, British, European societies are materially

and psychologically shaped by their historical and ongoing imperialisms. The need for
profit and the need to avoid understanding
colonial structures, and what they make of
the people who run and live in them, remain
mutually reinforcing. Palestine is pres-
ent-day imperialism's laboratory, in the last
region of the world to be formally colonized
and occupied by Western empires. This places it—its subjugation and its resistance—in
direct relation to any question of liberation
almost anywhere. Our solidarity cannot be
made—and it is an act of creation—from
a position of passive witnessing, and it
cannot be bracketed from the rest of life. My
solidarity with Palestine must be a practice
that is also about me, and my life, and my
future, and that of my children.

Despite the tremendous effort to isolate
and diminish Palestine physically, geograph-
ically, and as an idea, it has always garnered
the solidarity of most of the world's people
because the world's majority *are* the people
surviving displacement, war, surveillance,
incarceration, restricted movement, and
ethnonationalism. Today's unprecedented
mobilization of cross-movement solidarity
with Palestine in the United States and
other parts of the world demonstrates that
people also understand that Palestinians are
being dominated *in the same ways and with
the same visions and technologies* as the
majority of us. The connections built and
made between decolonial struggles of the
last century and through to the Black Lives
Matter and Indigenous rights movements
of recent years are helping propel a historic
shift in people's understandings and positions on Palestine, and Israel.

These essays, which were written and
edited before the October seventh attacks
on Israel by Hamas fighters from Gaza,
can help carry us through the rupture and
the overwhelming violence of this moment
to a solidarity that is clear-eyed about its
shared stakes, to a commitment to act now
while holding a longer view. On these pages
is Palestine as part of the world, alive and
connected to other places, ideas, cities, and
struggles. In their approach and engagement,
the essays reflect a shift in the Palestine
Festival of Literature (PalFest), which has
brought hundreds of writers and artists
from around the world to Palestine since
2008. PalFest has always been an act of
solidarity and over time it has moved from
a post-Intifada, pre-social media focus on
witnessing and exposure to a festival that is
about an exchange of ideas and experiences
from across the Global South, in Palestine.
The aim is to enable work towards mutual
freedom, which is the only kind we can
hope for.

This book is not for readers to understand Palestine, although it will impart
some knowledge about that place. It is for
readers to better understand themselves,
their futures, and how they might fight for
them. ●

MAHDI SABBAGH

Introduction

RENEWING SOLIDARITY

"How can you live in this place?" shouted our history and geography teacher, entering our tenth-grade classroom.[1] "I do not understand how anyone can live like this!" She was late, flustered, and, as we soon learned, had just crossed a checkpoint where Israeli soldiers had harassed her. Although she was not Palestinian, she had chosen to live in a Palestinian neighborhood in Jerusalem during the depths of the second Intifada, and her experience at the checkpoint reflected a daily occurrence for her Palestinian students. She was right to be angry: the ways our lives were endangered, our environment besieged and reduced to a military experiment, were hard to bear.

At that moment, she had the option to pack up and leave Jerusalem. But she returned to our classroom daily, and crossed the checkpoint daily, until we had all passed our *baccalauréat* and graduated. The simple, inconceivable act of staying in Palestine exemplified solidarity as it's typically discussed: a foreigner eschewed many easier lifestyles to live among us, choosing to contribute to our community despite its many challenges. But solidarity was a way of life that we as Palestinians already understood intimately. We protected each other on the streets, on buses, in schools, at checkpoints. Solidarity was and continues to be a collective culture in which we're raised and a code of ethics that we continue to practice. Perhaps those who visited or moved to Palestine to be with us hadn't brought solidarity with them but had simply learned how to be Palestinian.

Many of us carry sensibilities of solidarity in our day-to-day life. We know when to hide, but also when to render ourselves visible in order to support each other. We develop languages—textual, oral, and bodily; through symbolism, through image, through sound—that make the political legible. The genesis of this volume lay in the questions I asked of my own subjectivity in relation to solidarity, and soon enough that inquiry encompassed a plurality of knowledge based on the infinitely diverse experiences of its authors. Solidarities and the many forms they can take are always new, because they require constant renewal, updating, adjusting in order to move side by side with struggles and movements. *Their Borders, Our World* is a reflection on what we perhaps already know because we are in it daily, attempting to make sense of the great struggles—but also the great possibilities—that come when we stand beyond the limitations imposed on our imaginations to be in solidarity with each other.

"Thank you for resisting the invitation to dance on our graves,"[2]
or Making Choices Under Siege
To step outside the distinctly complex negotiations central to Palestinian life for a moment, writing about, and thinking clearly within, our dystopian reality is not a simple task. The term "burnout" has become inadequate to describe the level of emotional exhaustion that individuals and communities face as they grapple with the ongoing pandemic, the clearer-than-ever disposability of our lives, and the devaluing of our labor.

The Covid-19 pandemic, of course, isn't the culprit; it merely slipped comfortably into the gaps of our societies and made them larger, more visible, more concrete, harder to patch. Inequality, we keep repeating to ourselves, is at an all-time high in virtually every sector of society. Inequality is discussed as a condition to be remedied by policies, by law, by economics, by taxes, by charity, by capital. But those who cannot make ends meet, whose livelihoods and lives are violated, experience inequality not as a bureaucratic operation but as injustice, as a continuous siege. The pandemic, and governments' kneejerk reactions to it, besieged communities already dispossessed by capitalism's extractive properties. This is where relationality steps in as a tactical remedy to this condition: it calls for us to come together. But drawing connections between different realities—each of which grapples with inequality differently—can be difficult and reductive, prone to an infinity of errors. And yet, my hope is that this very act, of drawing connections, can lead to novel possibilities, maybe even solutions.

Because I come from Jerusalem, I have learned to see injustice vividly, often to my own detriment and sometimes even erroneously. It has been ingrained in me since my birth in a city under siege where the oppression of a colonized people is visible to the most untrained of naked eyes: from the daily violence inflicted on Palestinian youth by Israeli soldiers at Damascus Gate, to the policing and harassment of Palestinian bodies at dozens of now permanently constructed checkpoints, to the planning policies that expropriate Palestinian lands and that refuse to give out building permits, then send in the bulldozers when Palestinians build.

Much like in Manu Karuka's framework on the North American continent, Palestine is reduced to a state of "frontier," where a suspension of morals and ethics allows the allegedly democratic government, benefiting corporations, businesses, and individual settlers to cross "the line from civilization to savagery" with complete impunity.[3] In the case of Palestine, this frontier, of course, isn't a line but a spatial condition that occurs whenever Israeli settler colonialism approaches a Palestinian space, Palestinian built environment, or Palestinian body. But far from inducing despair (how much injustice can our societies put up with?) this has made me attuned to settler colonialism's banality—the banality of its architecture, of its predictable similarity wherever humans might inflict it. This hyperawareness to injustice in settler-colonial formations is the backdrop for my own subjectivity. In New York, from which I am writing this reflection, injustice is also painfully visible, albeit in very different contexts than in Jerusalem. It is visible in the movement of people through the city's gentrifying neighborhoods. Simply walk down any street and observe the contrast in people's lives: Who commutes at 6:00 a.m.? Who gets to work from home or from a coffeeshop? Who delivers food to whose door? Who takes the subway, who drives, who gets driven? There are infinite examples of inequity's everyday manifestations that need not be listed here to acknowledge that they also (when applied systemically) result in a condition where injustice dominates. Instead, the fundamental questions through which I would like to frame this reflection are: What does one do, how does one act, and where does one position oneself vis-à-vis the banality

of inequality, vis-à-vis injustice? While this volume doesn't directly answer the questions here, it uses them as a backdrop to explore solidarity with and from Palestine.

This volume floats in the flows of liberatory ideas that come from under and in spite of settler-colonial geographies. It understands solidarity as a collective work in progress with immense potential and possibility for a liberated, just future. Solidarity—coming or acting together based on or in order to achieve a shared set of goals and principles—has been at the heart of the Palestine Festival of Literature (PalFest), itself the product of a network of writers and thinkers concerned with Palestine. Solidarity has always been there, explicitly and implicitly, and this volume invites us to discuss solidarity as an epistemology. Good solidarity work is continuous: it doesn't cease to move and expand; it builds, it amasses people and knowledge. In his 2008 letter to the Palestine Festival of Literature, which was published in the 2017 volume *This Is Not a Border*, Mahmoud Darwish describes solidarity visits to Palestine as "an expression of what Palestine has come to mean to the living human conscience."[4] For Darwish, visiting Palestine for the exclusive sake of being in solidarity is an act of engagement, of understanding one's role, of truth-searching. Many of the essays in this book directly and indirectly propose ways of doing, acting, and positioning, both taking Darwish's letter to heart and proving that the letter's call is well and alive.

The Palestinian people have never ceased to struggle for the liberation of our lands and built environments. However, at least prior to October 2023, promises and tactics proposed by old leadership—in the occupied territories, but also in 1948 Palestine (Israel)—have failed because, simply put, that leadership has profited from gradual Israeli settler-colonialist expansion on Palestinian houses, lands, and resources. Scholar Ahmad El Hirbawi pointed to how the Palestinian public, at least in 2022, had largely ceased to see its single-party political leadership in Gaza and the West Bank as representative of or effective in communal and political life; against the will of the public, the leadership had instead defaulted to tribalism, meaning to modes of governance based on loyalty to political parties.[5] This observation was written prior to the genocidal war on Gaza, whose political, human, environmental, psychological, and moral ramifications we have yet to fully comprehend. What we do understand is that it has eclipsed much of what we believed and simultaneously provided us with a painful clarity that we are not safe from genocide. This ongoing Nakba propels us to organize even more, and proudly. The 2021 Unity Intifada rendered clear to many that Palestinians, and especially young Palestinians, have been shifting their collective discourse toward new grassroots narratives and directions throughout 1948 Palestine, the West Bank, the Gaza Strip, refugee camps across the Arab world, and the diaspora beyond. On the ground, this shift is seen in the pluralization of activist voices coming from Sheikh Jarrah, Silwan, Gaza, Haifa, Nazareth, and the Naqab, but also importantly in growing ties to other liberatory movements across the planet, such as the Black Lives Matter and NoDAPL movements and other Indigenous and landed struggles. Today's conditions

of settler colonialism in Palestine are as dire as ever, but even a genocide could not crush the poetry of Refaat Alareer, who was martyred on December 6, 2023, in Gaza. His gargantuan words, "If I must die / . . . / let it be a tale," ricochet through cities across the planet in solidarity with Palestine.

In fact, central to the Palestinian struggle is the telling and retelling of tales, stories, memories that are both real and imagined. There is a veritable sprouting of new Palestinian critical perspectives on our history and geography, embodied in archival projects such as حكايا غزة (*Gaza Story*); Grassroots Al-Quds; Sabil Library; Rasha Salti and Kristine Khouri's *Past Disquiet: Narratives and Ghosts from the International Art Exhibition for Palestine, 1978*; the Palestinian Museum Digital Archive; Mohanad Yaqubi (Subversive Film)'s *Tokyo Reels*; Lama Suleiman's *Parallax Haifa*; Danah Abdulla and Sarona Abuaker's *Countless Palestinian Futures*; Skin Deep's *Palestine: Ways of Being*, curated by Zena Agha; and Lifta Volumes. These and many other projects begin to suggest a diversification of liberatory narratives that reformulate existing archives, build archives where there are none, and infuse Palestinian history with feminist ideologies and futurism. This, in turn, produces a potentiality for many futures for Palestine, despite an entrenching settler-colonial apparatus. Throughout this long political shift, the praxis of solidarity appears like a thread, weaving through different movements back and forth and enabling the exchange of ideas, tactics, and tools.

In *Time-Space Colonialism*, Juliana Hu Pegues studies Asian laborers' and Indigenous Tlingit people's experiences in settler colonialism in Alaska.[6] Through their (forced) labor in canneries, each community has a window onto the other's commonality, and this, Hu Pegues shows, subsequently forms a potential bedrock for mutuality in solidarity. This potential lies in tapping into the possibility of solidarity from muddled and complex realities where it is infinitely easier to conform to the illusion of assimilation through hard labor—not having a choice in where you get displaced to but certainly having a choice in how you position yourself politically. The *Funambulist*'s numerous publications form another example of solidarity praxis, becoming an aggregate of writings that highlight liberation activism and fuel solidarity work. Jewish American allies and Boycott, Divestment, Sanctions (BDS) activists such as those in Jewish Voice for Peace (JVP) enact through their work a future possibility that Zionism categorically denies us. Coerced or performative coexistence runs amok and typically upholds severely unequal sharing of power and resources—a "peacewashing." But JVP's important work, on the contrary, not only assists and complements the liberatory narratives coming out of Palestine but also fundamentally enacts a future inevitability of pluralism and genuine coexistence.

Solidarity with Palestine is, of course, a decades-long project. In their research and exhibition work, curators Kristine Khouri and Rasha Salti touch on the *International Art Exhibition for Palestine*, organized by the Palestine Liberation Organization (PLO) in 1978 in Beirut. The exhibition was an important culmination of art and media with the dual function of garnering solidarity and educating a Palestinian and larger Arab population on the struggle. It also had international ambitions: parts of the exhibition traveled to Japan, then to Iran, then to Norway.[7] Khouri and Salti describe solidarity as simultaneously "an incarnation" and "a projection."[8] Grassroots solidarity work here led to a larger cultural project that benefited the PLO, and Khouri and Salti remind us that "the first pillar of international solidarity with the Palestinian struggle was spontaneous, grassroots pan-Arab mobilization."[9] Solidarity is a possibility harnessed by both organizational bodies and grassroots movements, and, ultimately, solidarity is a tool available to us all, as individuals, as collectives, as families, and as communities. Remembering historical solidarity, pondering the relationalities that result from solidarity, and tapping into a contemporary web of solidarity thought is perhaps an attempt to exist in this world, for many of us marginalized and violated by the day-to-day violence of existing structures of power.

Witnessing

A fundamental precursor for solidarity building is the act of witnessing. It is certainly possible to understand settler colonialism in Palestine by reading, looking at maps, and so on. But witnessing—what Gil Hochberg calls "countervisual practice" that undermines "Israeli visual dominance"—allows us to visualize what, in the case of Palestine, is often unfathomable injustice.[10] Through her study of photography and Palestinian art, Alessandra Amin reminds us that to "bear witness" to Palestinian suffering from outside of Palestine constitutes a gaze that can "substitute the impotent and voyeuristic act of looking for meaningful intervention against the atrocities depicted."[11] Witnessing

9

by itself is in fact futile. Witnessing must
be integrated into a practice of solidarity to
formulate meaningful change. To witness
injustice, seared into the landscape, into
the built environment, allows the mind
to ask a cascade of questions: How do
people experience injustice? Why are they
subjugated to injustice? Who designed this
injustice? How was it funded? Who benefits
from it? Witnessing the built environment
helps us begin to tackle these questions,
as the answer lies right in front of us. As
entrenched and complex as settler colonialism might seem at first, the forms in which
it manifests itself spatially are self-evident,
their function mundanely obvious.

In Palestine, as in other geographies
plagued by settler colonialism, witnessing
has become an ingrained tradition. It is a
skill we pick up shortly after birth. We learn
to cry, to eat, to walk, and then to witness.
During the second Intifada, we were
mostly locked up at home in Beit Hanina,
Jerusalem. In 2004, on a cool summer night,
my father called me to go with him to the
roof of our apartment building. From the
roof he pointed in the direction of Ramallah:
"Look." You could see Ramallah's dark
skyline (like us in East Jerusalem, they had
also lost electricity) and every few minutes
a bright flash of light would fall from the
sky onto the buildings, followed by a long,
faint boom. I will always remember this day
as a lesson in witnessing. The importance is
to pay attention, to turn to where the crime
is happening, to observe, to remember.
Witnessing is perhaps important because
it acts as a foundation for undeniability, a
foundation on which one can begin to reach
out once the violence has paused. A foundation for solidarity.

Witnessing is also an act that can help solidify an existing understanding of injustice. Maybe we ought to understand witnessing as an active approach, not a passive one. During the 2020 Black Lives Matter uprising in the United States, protesters learned to pause and observe anytime a police officer stopped a Black individual on the street, sometimes through the cameras on their phones. It became, one would hope, common knowledge that it is one's civic responsibility to observe, to not turn one's back on an interaction that by its very design is an enactment of white supremacy. The documentation of state-sponsored brutality—as we have seen in St. Louis, in Standing Rock, in Cairo, in Hong Kong, in Jerusalem—not only becomes active witnessing but also suggests how savvy our societies have become at building bodies of evidence and disseminating them quickly. Through his work on mutual aid in moments of crisis, Dean Spade reminds us that "contact with the complex realities of injustice" eventually births a commitment to solidarity.[12]

Witnessing can also be applied as a spatial and visual lens to see buildings, streets, cities and how they operate and behave. Witnessing allows the witness to develop a spatial index of injustice. On a recent visit to the American Southwest, I went to visit the ancestral land of the O'odham and Piipaash people in Arizona. I was, of course, aware of their ongoing dispossession, but it wasn't until I saw Phoenix and the Salt River Pima-Maricopa Reservation that I understood what exactly dispossession looked like—and how hauntingly familiar it felt. Dispossession, here and elsewhere, is a condition that permeates all aspects of daily life and every granule of the built environment. Witnessing the stark contrast between the wealthy Scottsdale urban sprawl—manicured, desertscape lawns, serviced by golf courses and immaculately paved roads—and the Salt River Reservation's roadside trash and cracked asphalt roads revealed in just how many ways dispossession manifests itself spatially on the reservation. Settlement expanded throughout the 1800s, and then-president Rutherford B. Hayes's 1879 Executive Order established a 680,000-acre reservation that solidified and legalized settlement expansion by confining the Indigenous population. Later that year, Hayes signed another executive order that reduced the Salt River Reservation to just 46,627 acres, effectively cutting off the O'odham and Piipaash peoples from the majority of their land and access to the river that had been their source of food, culture, and identity, and making way for what became the city of Phoenix.[13] America is especially skilled at constructing inequality, and thresholds between unequal allocations of resources can be seen everywhere: from disparities in street and water infrastructure between Scottsdale and the Salt River Reservation, to how supermarkets and fresh produce are allocated along racial lines in New York's Hunts Point, to how access to abortion begins and ends along shifting invisible borders at the strike of a Supreme Court justice's pen. In actively witnessing what oppressive systems do to communities and their environments we begin to build a tradition of witnessing, one that makes solidarity not only possible but inevitable.

"Although I often feel lost on this trail, I know I am not alone,"[14]
or Mutuality
Solidarity with Palestine also inspired Palestinians to look outward toward the possibility of new coalitions: with other Indigenous people, with Black liberation, with movements to open borders. We have much in common with others who have been crushed by settler colonialism elsewhere, and this commonality can become mutual solidarity, or mutuality, if we act on it. This important political space, between silence and appropriation, is difficult and uncomfortable, as it perhaps should be. There is also a particular danger of diluting, of muddling, of confusing, that happens when we attempt to equate conditions across disparate timelines, disparate geographies, and disparate configurations of racial and colonial formations. Meaningful mutuality does not flatten this difference, nor does it accept its limitations and walk away; it instead recognizes difference and learns from it.

Kanaka Maoli activist and educator J. Kēhaulani Kauanui describes how in the 2019 mobilization to protect the sacred, living mountain of Mauna Kea in Hawai'i, solidarity in many forms poured in from neighboring islands and from around the globe and that the key was "responding to what people on the ground are calling for."[15] This can happen in many ways: by amplifying the voices of those on the ground, by using the language that they put forward, by respecting and solidifying their picket lines. Solidarity can only be effective in response to guidance from those directly affected, and when solidarity moves in both directions it becomes exponentially more powerful.

Mutuality is a tactic that first requires and then further enables communities to listen and learn from one another to form ideological ties, coalitions, and triangulations of knowledge exchange.[16] Mutuality is power.

Under our mutually devastated environments, one need not look far to find shared struggles and opportunities for mutuality. For example, although concerns of land and housing in Palestine (such as in Sheikh Jarrah and Silwan) and issues of houselessness in Indigenous communities on Turtle Island originated in different temporal, political, and social formations, people confronting these conditions could, in recognizing each other, learn from each other's perseverance.[17] Prisoner movements in Palestine and abolitionist ideology in Black communities and Indigenous communities in North America have much to learn from each other as well. One can imagine future possibilities for mutual learning between Palestine and endless other Indigenous geographies: Armenia, Kurdistan, Western Sahara, Haudenosaunee territory, Puerto Rico, Dinétah, Guatemala, Hawai'i, Aotearoa, among many others. The intention isn't to reduce liberatory struggles to abstractions or metaphors, nor is it to cover every ground, but to propose and demonstrate the infinite possibility of relating to one another, of mutualities yet to come.

Mutuality, of course, is already occurring. For example the Indigenous group the Red Nation has made a pledge of solidarity to Palestinian liberation, highlighting the important role of what they call "lateral solidarity" in the Indigenous liberation movement.[18] Their position paper "The Right of Return Is LANDBACK" makes clear connections between Palestine's Land Day, a day when Palestinians commemorate the expropriation of their land and the killing of their people in 1976 by the Israeli state, and LANDBACK, a call to give land back to Indigenous people on Turtle Island.[19] Another example is the slogan "No Ban on Stolen Land" deployed by Melanie Yazzie and Nick Estes at a protest against the Trump administration's Executive Order 13769, which banned travelers from several majority-Muslim countries. The slogan, and its subsequent viral spread on social media, called into question our understanding of borders imposed by settler states by instead turning to "migrant and refugee justice grounded in Indigenous sovereignty."[20] The decades-long relationship between South African and Palestinian anti-apartheid, grassroots movements has steadily grown in impact in recent decades. In July 2022, South Africa's minister of international relations and cooperation, Naledi Pandor, called for Israel to be designated an apartheid state. "As oppressed South Africans," she stated, "we experienced firsthand the effects of racial inequality, discrimination, and denial, and we cannot stand by while another generation of Palestinians are left behind."[21] The possibility for a different relationality, for kinship, occurs when we reach out and attempt to be in mutual solidarity. Palestinian American writer Steven Salaita calls this "inter/nationalism" and reminds us that this shift in thought, in practice, and in worldview can and should also occur in scholarship.[22]

Settler colonialism pushes colonized people into silos and forces them onto islands of resistance. Building mutuality reminds us that we in fact are not alone. Visual cues—for example, a large, hand-painted "NO DAPL" sign tucked behind a local eatery at the Salt River Reservation, a George Floyd mural painted on a destroyed building in Gaza City, the raising of an Algerian flag next to a Palestinian one over al-Aqsa Mosque or at a football game—all remind us of the power of mutual solidarity to transcend geographic distance and isolation. They remind us that our struggles are interconnected in a number of ways: not only are there multiple struggles occurring simultaneously against colonial regimes that behave with expected similarities, but also our traditions of resistance, or what Estes calls an "accumulation of resistance"[23] have the potential to be interconnected, to teach us, and to give us moral and ideological grounding on which to continue what often feels like an impossible task.

Still Steadfast, Still Persevering, or صمود

In the Palestinian context, this "accumulation of resistance" has a particular context: that of صمود (*sumud*), or steadfast perseverance. Palestinians have developed a collective praxis of resistance that has become ingrained and can be conceptualized in many ways. The practice of sumud is an ideological principle developed after the 1967 war, when the West Bank and Gaza Strip fell under Israeli occupation. Sumud suggests a third way of existing, beyond submission or exile.[24] Some practices of sumud look inward—for example, when one stays put on one's land.[25] This *static* sumud is a practice seen, for example, in Silwan and Sheikh Jarrah, where Palestinians' lives are made unlivable by Israel's policies of ethnic cleansing, as well as by settler

organizations that view Palestinian lives as disposable, as less than human. Palestinians' will and ability to stay in their homes despite daily harassment is a practice of sumud. This also appears in the acts of building and renovating homes. This *architectural* sumud is a defiant practice that puts the needs of the residents before the bureaucracy that illegalizes the very act of building on one's own land.[26]

Sumud can be practiced individually, but when practiced collectively it begins to also produce communal awareness. Practiced at the scale of an entire community, it is a sumud that aims to build political consciousness, establish relational bonds of care, and develop politically active communities. *Communal* sumud is especially critical because it has the ability to break down fear: fear of waving a Palestinian flag, fear of taking the Israeli municipality to court, fear of saying no to exploitation, fear of pushing back. After the 2014 kidnapping, torture, and murder of Mohammed Abu Khdeir by Israeli right-wing nationalists, his family did not have to deal with the tragedy alone: the entirety of Shu'fat and Beit Hanina rose in rebellion to protest the murder, creating a condition of high visibility that ultimately forced Israeli authorities to arrest and try the murderers. Jerusalem's Palestinians rose again, in unison, after the Israeli army executed Shireen Abu Akleh in 2022, forcing the world to witness and to react to the frontier condition that exposes the lack of democratic practices in Israel, but also warning the Israeli authorities that Palestinians will reject their assumed disposability and honor every living being. Protest, even when it might appear futile, is a practice of sumud. Another crucial example of communal sumud is seen in the ability of Gazans to remain alive and defiant despite the crushing Israeli-Egyptian blockade, the inadequate nutritional rations dictated by the blockade, and a total lack of accountability for Israeli war crimes committed during the almost annual military assaults on Gaza between 2006 and 2022.[27] Gaza practiced sumud through the Great Marches of Return, but also through the people's daily lives, constantly coming up with new solutions to cope with unfathomable conditions. Such practices of coming together in protest constitute communal sumud. These moments become critical in Palestinian teaching, in witnessing and rendering visible what Israel tries desperately to conceal abroad through elaborate public relations campaigns and as popular political education.

We typically think of sumud as a principle that one enacts on the land, in Palestine, under occupation. But what if repertoires of sumud are also useful to those who are not in Palestine, but who work toward justice in Palestine? Other critical practices of sumud look further afield, toward the world outside of historic Palestine. As more Palestinians find themselves in refugee camps, in the diaspora, in self-imposed exiles at all four corners of the planet, sumud takes on new forms, ones that reach outward and bring in allyships, networks of solidarity. What does it mean to hold on to sumud in exile? How does this relate to solidarity? Palestine activism is regularly suppressed and censored in the West, in ways that at times echo the suppression of freedom of expression and of political affiliation under direct Israeli rule. In exile, solidarity also requires steadfastness, the ability to continue to act in solidarity despite attempts at silencing and censorship. Sumud is an increasingly effective Palestinian praxis that latches on to solidarity and helps it build ties across the planet, reaching out to new locales, emboldening allies, and forming unprecedented connections with other struggles. This *global* sumud has historically, ironically been fueled by the forced exiles of Palestinian thinkers and activists who learned to be steadfast under Israeli rule first. For example, in 1970 Sabri Jiryis was forced out of historic Palestine and resettled in Beirut. Instead of stopping his activism, he brought his political knowledge from the Land Movement (Al Ard) to the PLO's work in Lebanon. His exile, far from ending his sumud, intensified it—now as an outward-facing tactic that allowed him to take part in a nascent network of solidarity. Global sumud teaches us that one need not be in Palestine, or even Palestinian, to remain steadfast in solidarity with Palestine.

This volume takes this question further by asking whether tactics of steadfast perseverance can be helpful when adopted by other communities that work toward decolonization, wherever they might be. With mutuality in mind, the volume also asks whether Palestinians in their sumud can learn from Black and Indigenous societies and their tactics of survival and resistance. What might a kind of sumud that learns from other struggles and returns to Palestine with a more expanded repertoire of resistance look like?

Writing on Solidarities as "Poetic Knowledge"[28]

While the catalyst of this volume was the May 2021 Palestinian Unity Intifada, much of the writing and editing work occurred closer to the assassination of Shireen Abu Akleh, another act of heinous colonial violence that garnered immense international solidarity with Palestine across the planet.

Nevertheless, this volume is not to be understood as a response to a specific event, year, or phase of settler colonialism, but rather as a reflection that can travel back and forth in time with the ebbs and flows of resistance movements. Perhaps it can aim to be added to the Palestinian critical perspectives mentioned above, and hope to be understood, in the words of Robin D. G. Kelley, as "poetic knowledge," meaning an imagination, an effort to see future possibility in the present. Kelley reminds us that "things need not always be this way."[29]

Israel exports techniques and technologies of war and biopolitical governmentality (of debilitation) to the world,[30] and Palestine becomes the testing ground for resistance, for life, for cultural production, and for global solidarities in the seams of nation-states and at the peripheries of state-sanctioned narratives. What Palestine can offer the world is a manual for *means*: means for twenty-first-century life, for kinship, for hiding, for survival under extreme disparities of wealth and harsh environmental conditions. This increasingly vital knowledge is not always tangible or written. It is produced once we practice relationality and solidarity work.

Although some of the thinkers who tirelessly contributed here experienced Palestine through PalFest's 2019 festival, this volume became a reality once I reached out to them two years later with a prompt on solidarity and its future. It is difficult to write about violence, let alone to build solidarity knowledge in the face of it, when its pain is fresh in one's mind. The hope is that the various essays of this volume are legible to our readers in any and all stages of witnessing structural violence, attempting mutuality work, and practicing sumud.

The ten authors you will read here each cover a world of ideas. In contributions loosely grouped in three parts, Choices under Siege, Witnessing, and Mutuality, the authors share their political choice-making, their perceptive vision, and their efforts at mutual understanding. When we begin to ask questions, how do we confront the need to take difficult political stances? Keller Easterling takes deep cuts through time to encourage us to try to be in Palestine. Tareq Baconi takes us to Gaza where he asks us to confront the abject. Dina Omar embarks on the difficult journey of unlearning by seeing the ways Palestinians are perpetually gaslit by those who uphold structural power today. How do we make sense of the destruction, of the uprooting, of the pain that we witness? Samia Henni takes us back in time to look at records that expose French and Israeli practices of nuclear destruction in the colonized deserts of Algeria and Palestine. Omer Shah takes us back and forth between the holy sanctuaries of Islam and the hegemonies of power that coerce them. Kareem Rabie shows us how people form identities within worlds of capitalist alienation in which exile is often inevitable. Given this seemingly impossible reality, how is mutuality then constructed? Ellen van Neerven intimately gears us through the possibility of surviving unfathomable erasure together. Omar Robert Hamilton stitches Cairo and Jerusalem together, reflecting on the urban changes transforming both cities into ugly, hypersurveilled, anti-cities. Mabel O. Wilson, through her attentive eyes, teaches us how to read the violence of architecture, leaving us with the guiding words of Frantz Fanon.

This anthology in no way claims to function as a complete aggregate of solidarities, as that would be impossible. It should instead be understood as a humble contribution to an increasingly expanding web of solidarity thought that connects archipelagos severed from each other by design. Read this volume as an instigation, a call to continue to think differently. Read it for its proposed language, proposed analysis, proposed futures that might help us continue to weave this web of defiance that relentlessly grabs the attention of the fragile and insecure power structures of planetary settler colonialism. Read it as a catalyst for connections, a window into the propelling world of possibilities that solidarities grant us. ●

ENDNOTES

1. My use of the pronouns "we," "us," and "ours" here and later in this introduction refer to a collective state of being Palestinian. Many of the events we, as Palestinians, go through—such as crossing a checkpoint—are experienced as a collective.

2. Mahmoud Darwish, "Welcome," in *This Is Not a Border: Reportage & Reflection from the Palestine Festival of Literature*, ed. Ahdaf Soueif and Omar Robert Hamilton (New York: Bloomsbury, 2017), 9.

3. Manu Karuka, *Empire's Tracks: Indigenous Nations, Chinese Workers, and the Transcontinental Railroad* (Berkeley: University of California Press, 2019), 169.

4. Darwish, "Welcome," 7.

5. Suleiman Abu Arshid, Discussion | The Palestinian Authority between state failure and a return to tribalism, Arab 48 Online, July 26, 2022.
[سليمان أبو ارشيد، حوار | السلطة الفلسطينية بين فشل الدولة وعودة القبيلة، عرب ٤٨]

6. Juliana Hu Pegues, *Space-Time Colonialism: Alaska's Indigenous and Asian Entanglements* (Chapel Hill: University of North Carolina Press, 2021).

7. Kristine Khouri & Rasha Salti, eds., *Past Disquiet: Artists, International Solidarity and Museums in Exile* (Museum of Modern Art in Warsaw, 2019), 33.

8. Khouri and Salti, *Past Disquiet*, 21.

9. Khouri and Salti, *Past Disquiet*, 20.

10. Gil Z. Hochberg, *Visual Occupations: Violence and Visibility in a Conflict Zone* (Durham, NC: Duke University Press, 2015), 8.

11. Alessandra Amin, "'A Treasury of Rays': Finding a Winter Garden in Palestine," in "Family Photographs," ed. Deepali Dewan, special issue, *Trans Asia Photography* 9, no. 1 (Fall 2018), http://hdl.handle.net/2027/spo.7977573.0009.103.

12. Dean Spade, *Mutual Aid: Building Solidarity during This Crisis (and the Next)* (London: Verso, 2020), 15.

13. This history is laid out in detail in the permanent displays of the Huhugam Ki Museum in the Salt River Reservation in so-called Phoenix, Arizona.

14. Layli Long Soldier, *Whereas* (Minneapolis: Graywolf Press, 2017), 50.

15. Quoted in Lou Cornum, "Fight for the Future: On Mauna Kea Hundreds Are Holding a Refuge and Defending Land from the Proponents of False Progress," *New Inquiry*, August 2, 2019, https://thenewinquiry.com/fight-for-the-future/.

16. Cornum, "Fight for the Future."

17. See The Red Nation, *The Red Deal: Indigenous Action to Save Our Earth* (Brooklyn: Common Notions Press, 2021), 55, 81.

18. The Red Nation, "The Liberation of Palestine Represents an Alternative Path for Native Nations," Samidoun: Palestinian Prisoner Solidarity Network, September 17, 2019, https://samidoun.net/2019/09/the-red-nation-the-liberation-of-palestine-represents-an-alternative-path-for-native-nations/.

19. NDN Collective, "The Right of Return Is LANDBACK," https://ndncollective.org/right-of-return-is-landback/.

20. Harshita Yalamarty, "Lessons from 'No Ban on Stolen Land,'" *Studies in Social Justice* 14, no. 2 (2021): 476.

21. Thabi Menya, "South Africa Calls for Israel to Be Declared an 'Apartheid State,'" *Al Jazeera*, July 26, 2022, https://www.aljazeera.com/news/2022/7/26/south-africa-calls-for-israels-proscription-as-apartheid-state.

22. Steven Salaita, *Inter/Nationalism: Decolonizing Native America and Palestine* (Minneapolis: University of Minnesota Press, 2016), 170.

23. Nick Estes, *Our History Is the Future: Standing Rock Versus the Dakota Access Pipeline, and the Long Tradition of Indigenous Resistance* (London: Verso, 2019), 167.

24. Mahdi Sabbagh, "Sumud: Repertoires of Resistance in Silwan," *Public Culture* 34, no. 3 (2022), https://doi.org/10.1215/08992363-9937396.

25. Samih K. Farsoun and Jean M. Landis, "Structures of Resistance and the 'War of Position': A Case Study of the Palestinian Uprising," *Arab Studies Quarterly* 11, no. 4, (1989): 76.

26. Sabbagh, "Sumud."

27. See Tareq Baconi, "Wretched Gaza: Confronting the Abject" in this volume.

28. Robin D. G. Kelley, *Freedom Dreams: The Black Radical Imagination* (Boston: Beacon Press, 2002), 9.

29. Kelley, *Freedom Dreams*, 9.

30. Jasbir Puar, *The Right to Maim: Debility, Capacity, and Disability* (Durham, NC: Duke, 2017), 153. See also Yaniv Kubovich, "Israeli Arms Exports Spike 30%, Hit All-Time High," *Haaretz*, April 12, 2002, https://www.haaretz.com/israel-news/2022-04-12/ty-article/.premium/israels-arms-exports-hit-record-high-in-2021/00000180-5b94-d718-afd9-dfbc36710000.

JEHAN BSEISO

GAZA
LOVESONG

I go to Erez to remind myself that Gaza is now an angry ball of flames behind the wall,
my eyes shut, fingers move on their own to
read the sky in braille.
The clouds are pocked with fire balloons, they burn my fingers up.

I don't know how many times I died on the way to this place but never arrived.
(this)
You call to say: even the dead grow old without a homeland.
(this is)
You call to say: we cross the borders with our blood.
(this is how)
The air, it's full of children's songs, look

        Up

(this is how we set the siege on fire)

An earlier version of this poem was published in the *Funambulist* 25 (September–October 2019).

KELLER EASTERLING

TRY TO BE
IN PALESTINE

S tories of activist solidarity frequently
rewind to the 1960s and '70s—the
moment when the Pan-African, civil
rights, Non-Aligned, and Tricontinental
movements intertwined to generate complex
international relays of people and ideas. The
movements arguably flowered because of
how well they matched and countered the
confused conundrums of sovereignty exercised by the colonizing and globalizing of
imperial powers masquerading as nations.[1]
The victims of these oscillating sovereignties also exercised exceptional forms of
sovereignty—sometimes taking the form of
a state and sometimes finding strength in an
atomized presence. But the movements, led
in part by developing countries in the Global
South, arguably also failed because, at the

neoliberal turn, the Global North managed
to manipulate the very same conundrums to
acquire extra shape-shifting powers while
breaking South-South solidarity.

Palestine has been partially shaped
within these conundrums. It has been
continually invaded by a nation created
for a diaspora and backed by Western
superpowers, but diplomatic offerings are
still presented in terms of realist politics and
bounded nation-states. Or there are only the
cold-blooded offerings of the captor to its
captives—those of political superbugs who
embody some of these extra shape-shifting
powers and seem to be inoculated against
consequence. Palestine, adopting and at
times embodying some of the creative
sovereignties of 1960s and '70s international

solidarity, remains both a situated territory that cannot be relinquished and an atomized nation—a diaspora of supportive international activist networks.

PalFest maintains some of the elegant repertoires of international solidarity from the 1960s and '70s. But it also explores a broader repertoire capable of facing the recent, ever more treacherous and untraceable surges of capitalizing, colonizing, and globalizing since the neoliberal turn. In this moment, prevailing ideological positions provide insufficient preparation, and the political superbugs have also managed to pass off some of the dangers to nonhuman atmospheres with larger environmental consequences. How might an activist repertoire not only match but also exceed and overwhelm the sovereignties of contemporary dominant powers? Do the greater dangers they pose ironically inspire or even empower another, more robust form of solidarity—a planetary solidarity that prevailing powers cannot evade or subdue?

Return to that mid-twentieth-century moment of international solidarity and animate just a few of the most familiar stories again. Although this complex history has been told with vivid detail and synthesis by many others, a fast-forward even between moments in a bare outline is sufficient to see the sovereignties mixing—to see how movements are catalyzed, diluted, or concentrated at various junctures or how some terms circulating between struggles become pivotal or contagious.[2]

Turning the tables on colonizing powers, the advocacies of W. E. B. Du Bois, Marcus Garvey's Universal Negro Improvement Association, and a series of five international Pan-African conferences from 1900 to 1945 called for a transnational sovereignty for Black people for whom slavery had already created a forced global diaspora. When linked together, Pan-Africanism, Black nationalism, and US civil rights organizations acquired sufficient strength and international scope to bolster Afro-Asian solidarity emerging from the 1955 Bandung Asian-African meetings and the Non-Aligned Movement (NAM) in 1961.

Activists, intellectuals, artists, musicians, and other celebrities joined elected leaders as the ambassadors and delegates of this special sovereignty. Du Bois, C. L. R. James, Aimé Césaire, Frantz Fanon, Richard Wright, Eric Williams, George Padmore, and others provided an electrifying literature. Sukarno, Josip Broz Tito, Kwame Nkrumah, Jawaharlal Nehru, and Gamal Abdel Nasser created places of pilgrimage within the decolonizing wave of the 1950s and '60s. A year after Nkrumah was elected president of an independent Ghana in 1960, Accra had become such a destination. And the remarkable detail noted in many versions of this familiar story: as if embodying the shifting sovereignties of the moment, Du Bois had moved to Ghana and was living there until his death on August 28, 1963—the very day of the March on Washington.

The participants organized additional collective entities and convened in a variety of headquarters, assembly buildings, hotels, nightclubs, and arenas for conferences as well as cultural festivals and concerts. Tito's UN-style secretariat portrayed the Non-Aligned Movement as a power to rival the West. Nkrumah's Organization for African Unity (OAU) hoped to foster international solidarities among African states. In 1959, Malcolm X visited Africa and Asia as a representative of the Nation of Islam (NOI), and, after departing from the NOI in 1964, he traveled again across Africa and the Middle East.[3] In the same year, inspired by the OAU, he established an Organization for African American Unity (OAAU) that invited global leaders to the Audubon Ballroom in Harlem. Also in 1964, the United Nations Conference on Trade and Development (UNCTAD) and the Group of 77 (G-77) were established as the bureaucratic governance organs potentially capable of making the necessary deals for more equality between the Global North and South.

The 1966 Tricontinental Conference in Havana further consolidated a truly global resistance to imperialism and US bullying in the Americas. The Organization of Solidarity with the People of Asia, Africa, and Latin America (OSPAAAL) and its *TRIcontinental* magazine were clearinghouses of movements and conflicts around the world, in Vietnam, Guinea-Bissau, and Palestine, as Zionism was increasingly associated with US-backed imperialism. Activists circulating in these conflicts were present in its pages, and the magazine's graphics served as supporting posters all around the world.[4] Among the most unusual agents of international sovereignty, Che Guevara, who had delivered a speech to the United Nations in 1964, was something like a one-man military attaché or general available to initiate or lead in any struggle giving fight to superpowers.

The festivals and conferences continued as a cultural revolution was broadcast around the world from the satellites and devices of a globalizing media. Sun Ra,

Miriam Makeba, Youssou N'Dour, and too many others to mention were mixing with rock, folk, and freedom songs playing on the radio. Newsreel, later Third World Newsreel, was established in 1967 in New York City to report news from the other side of the world and the other side of national or imperial agendas.[5] While NASA was putting a man on the moon in 1969, PANAF, the first Pan-African festival in Algiers, was also looking at the planet from a new perspective.

After Nkrumah was deposed in 1964, attention had shifted from Ghana to Tanzania. President Julius K. Nyerere's Arusha Declaration of 1967 announced a socialist policy of *Ujamaa*, or familyhood, that established villages and cultural organizations in keeping with precolonial Indigenous culture. Tanzania hosted the Sixth Pan-African Conference in 1974, further strengthening Dar es Salaam as a new destination for global gatherings and pilgrimages of Black leaders, including Angela Davis and members of the Congress of Racial Equality (CORE) and the Student Nonviolent Coordinating Committee (SNCC).[6] Guyanese historian Walter Rodney, author of *How Europe Underdeveloped Africa* (1972), and Shirley Graham Du Bois were headquartered there. Rodney forged a link between Dar es Salaam and Atlanta, Georgia, where the Institute of the Black World had become a crossroads of Black thinkers and activists, among them Sylvia Wynter.[7]

Meanwhile, as the US Federal Bureau of Investigation's COINTELPRO targeted Black leaders, they ironically intensified this international networking. Kwame Ture (Stokely Carmichael), former SNCC chairman, Black Power advocate, and "honorary prime minister" of the Black Panther Party, lived in exile in Guinea with Nkrumah. Robert F. Williams, COINTELPRO exile and author of *Negroes with Guns*, moved between Cuba, Vietnam, China, and Tanzania for nearly a decade.[8] Broadcast from Havana, Williams's *Radio Free Dixie* mixed jazz with news of struggles around the world. In another astonishing construction of sovereignty, while still in Tanzania, Williams was named the first president of the Republic of New Afrika, a proposed nation of Louisiana, Mississippi, Alabama, Georgia, and South Carolina that would be based on the principles of Ujamaa.[9]

Through the United Nations Conference on Trade and Development and the G-77, leaders in the Global South—Nyerere primary among them—proposed a New International Economic Order in 1974 that would establish greater equity between the North and the South. The *Brandt Commission Report* of 1980 warned of the consequences of continued inequality, now expressed in terms of the survival of the planet. But the Thatcher and Reagan administrations managed to block reforms and even strengthen what would become known as the "Washington Consensus." The subsequent South Commission that Nyerere led outlined a program for South-South cooperation. But *The Challenge of the South: The Report of the South Commission* came out in 1990, just as it seemed that the West had won the Cold War and the so-called free market had triumphed. Even worse, the report came out as Saddam Hussein invaded Kuwait and the US was revving up its military engines around delusions of saving the world and protecting its stake in oil.[10]

Finally, the G-77 was no match for the G7. The established powers were too entrenched and too good at positioning themselves to be the beneficiaries of tilted playing fields while congratulating themselves for beneficence and eventually for post–Cold War liberation and prosperity. They used the Bretton Woods institutions designed to remedy financial causes of conflict to create a manipulated market claiming to be a free market. When their own economies were threatened, they worked to break solidarities in the Global South. The Organization of the Petroleum Exporting Countries (OPEC)'s responses

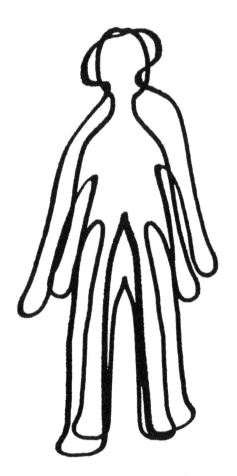

to US support for Israel had been a strong hand, but the West flexed their muscles to get OPEC to deal more favorably. And by raising the interest rate on debt to address inflation partly related to oil, the West returned developing countries to dependent relationships. The only way to pay the debt was to follow Washington Consensus rules and enter business relationships in the free-zone engine rooms of neoliberalism. And when substantial members of the NAM—China and the OPEC countries among them—deployed forms like free zones in ways that mimicked the West, they also arguably led to breaks in South-South solidarity.[11]

No single fast-forward through this moment—what Adom Getachew has called an episode of "worldmaking" activism—can do it justice.[12] But you can tell another story about the solidarities between the Pan-African, civil rights, Non-Aligned, and Tricontinental movements featuring different markers and different figures. It too will likely conjure a rich panorama of transnational networks and novel organs of governance or sovereignty as well as a sense that multiple systemic agents, rather than military events, changed the ground under everyone's feet.

With some adaptations to a polycentric world, contemporary activism revives many of the techniques from the 1960s and '70s. The Zapatistas are both a local and an omni-distributed coalition fighting for Indigenous liberation in Chiapas. The World Social Forum represents another congress producing nonbinding declarations like the 2006 Bamako Appeal, which may struggle to get any leverage but nevertheless represent some degree of international consensus. Black Lives Matter follows in the internationalist tradition of Black activists of the 1960s and '70s with trips to Palestine, Cuba, and the UK.[13] Some of the very same coalitions, even some of the very same people, like Angela Davis, are there to declare solidarity again. In this tradition, PalFest carries on the essential practices of convening, witnessing, programming, and publishing, but they are asking questions about additional forms and capacities for solidarity in the aftermath of a neoliberal turn.

In that aftermath, there is no singular enemy. That would be too easy. It is worse than that. There is a spectrum of dangers from capitalism, fascism, racism, whiteness, caste, religious intolerance, xenophobia, sociopathic leadership, and countless other means of hoarding authoritarian power while oppressing others and abusing the planet. Still, the spectrum keeps forming familiar cocktails of whiteness, imperialism, settler colonialism, racialized capital, and labor abuse. And those sewing the clothes, mining the minerals, sitting on the exhausted land, or facing the fire and water are often people of color or other victims of the extremes of inequality.

With no elementary particle like a nation-state, many dilemmas are the result of nested and conflicting forms of sovereignty enacted by many players. Established, situated states and intergovernmental organizations protect fluid, mobile organizations that move like weather fronts across national boundaries, deploying financial instruments, legal exemptions, data monopolies, and spatial products to expand their territory. The secular myths of modernism mix with fabled myths of imperial conquest in a totemic marketplace.

Political superbugs—whether figures like Bibi, Trump, Modi, and Putin, or bulletproof commercial organizations of capital—manipulate many different props, spaces, and scrambled ideologies. Sometimes it does not matter what they are, but only that they are changeable and constantly refreshed.

There is reason enough to be out in the streets every day, pressuring these consolidated powers to relinquish their grip. Activism will always be advocating, marching, unionizing, rioting, sabotaging, boycotting, blockading, sanctioning, and divesting among many other things. But in addition to the conventional battlegrounds and barricades, the places of contestation are everywhere. And an ability to detect environmental violence—the temperament embedded in all spaces and organizations—only offers more reasons to fight.

But maybe a broader tradition practiced in the remarkable episodes of the 1960s and '70s also involves converting abuses into advantages—like converting a forced diaspora into Pan-Africanism or converting the excesses of COINTELPRO into strengthened networks of international solidarity. In this way, converting the superinsulated, superlubricated powers operating after a neoliberal turn may involve not the customary declarations of singular evils and singular solutions but a confrontation with the full spectrum of evils. Singularity reproduces the modern Enlightenment logics of the last five hundred years. Singularity makes it easier for the superbugs, with their many masks and lies, to manipulate temperaments and incite binary fights from which to harvest loyalties and claim self-defense. The more agile activists know how to double-cross the superbugs by occasionally starving them of

the fight they crave—thus not releasing but rather increasing the leveraging pressure. It is the mixture of multiple techniques that is crucial to dissensus—dissensus with the capacity to keep power disoriented.

Maintaining multiple situated and atomized sovereignties strengthens this dissensus in a contemporary context. And nascent in the 1960s and '70s, but circulating more robustly with multiple contemporary struggles, references to indigeneity and planetary scales may also offer additional ways to convert the full spectrum of dangers into extra powers and solidarities.

As multiple sovereignties and coalitions thicken, Indigenous, Black, anarchist, abolitionist, and feminist victims of modern Enlightenment whiteness continue to offer increasingly powerful counterlogics. Sylvia Wynter, who was moving in the rich networks of 1960s and '70s international activism, synthesizing writers like Fanon and Césaire, leads a way to so many others who have been working to dismantle dominant habits of mind.[14] Those habits are continually reproduced even when trying to resist or overturn them—like the activists who feed superbugs with singular evils and singular solutions. But focused less on mirroring and thus aggrandizing an opponent, Wynter wrote about a broad reenchantment of human potentials.[15]

Since property and capital were some of the most durable instruments of that modern Enlightenment mind, these counterlogics also continually return the extra powers of mutualism or commoning on land that is not regarded as property. Mutualism sheds the desire for the singular, the modular, or the elementary particle because it relies on the differences that generate value through interdependence. Just as planting one seed returns ten, these exchanges, often engaging the live crust of the earth, produce an excess or abundance that does not make sense to capital or property. Redoubling any resources given to them, these organizations constitute an infrastructure as worthy of funding as those of concrete and conduit.

Powers accrue within broadening coalitions around these land-based politics. This is the undercommons in which, paraphrasing Fred Moten, it is harder for dominant powers to steal our right to share.[16] This is Arturo Escobar's "convivial" interplay between humans and nonhumans in a pluriverse. It is a reflection of the South American philosophy of *buen vivir*—an amalgam of anticapitalist, feminist, Indigenous, and environmentalist approaches. This is the mutualism that aligns with the African tradition of *ubuntu*.[17] These are the "community economies" about which J. K. Gibson-Graham writes.[18] This is the commons that scholars like Peter Linebaugh and Marcus Rediker have chronicled as the prevailing approach to land before European colonization even in an Anglo tradition.[19] Referencing Indigenous practices of inhabiting the land, this is also the "mobility commons" about which Mimi Sheller writes, which exists as "a relational practice of heterogenous coming together in negotiated political alliance."[20] Commoning is not only a means to occupy a place, it is also a pattern of circulating ideas.

As was clear in the activism of the 1960s and '70s, the commons sometimes only exist as an archipelago surrounded by threatening powers but linked by a mobility commons. Indigenous peoples have routinely been corralled into an archipelago surrounded by encroaching property. After the Civil War, Black people congregated in the Black Belt of the southern United States but were preyed upon by surrounding whites. All around the world, cooperative experiments from the 1950s to the 1970s—the Ujamaa villages in Tanzania, the ejido land in Mexico, the *gramdan* movement in India, or the Black cooperative movement in the US South—were forced to shrink or disappear by hostile surrounding powers. Intolerance and xenophobia ghettoize and terrorize religious groups and migrating peoples. Infrastructures that should serve communities segregate and isolate them. But as international solidarities have strengthened, migrations and media form a mobility commons that can never be completely shut down. A mobility commons not only returns ten seeds for every one that is planted, it is a limitless resource that can always find a way to spread through ideas, practices, and unexpected forms of kinship.

And there seem to be yet more special powers associated with invoking a global "kaleidoscopic" understanding of indigeneity.[21] The term indigeneity as used by Palestinians comes with some caveats, and it has even been used by Zionists to justify Israeli expansion. But it nevertheless reverberates with all those around the world whose land was seized by conquest.[22] Palestinian protests have been linking arms with other victims of settler colonialism, of any race, tribe, or identity. This alliance is claimed in the streets in the West Bank, Gaza, and within 1948 Palestine (Israel) or repeated in the countless international conferences, Zoom meetings, and marches around the world.[23] The 2019 PalFest gathering also reflected the increased reference to indigeneity in Palestinian activism while building ongoing alliances with Indigenous groups.

But some within these broad alliances have taken the term even further. Considering the Black diaspora of slavery or migrants of other conflicts, Saidiya Hartman has suggested that indigeneity can be about "a certain kind of inhabitation of the land or relation to Earth." Indigeneity might be made, not in relation to a "political claim." You can be Indigenous wherever you are with "no natal claims" because, like the slaves who traveled with seeds in their hair, you have a relationship to the land that does not regard it as a possession.[24]

Similarly, Anna Tsing notes that indigeneity is associated with "rhetorics of sovereignty; narratives of pluriethnic autonomy; (and) environmental stewardship." And while there are only contradictory definitions of indigeneity, she notes that "in contrast to Enlightenment universals, international Indigenous politics opens a global politics in which inconsistency and contradiction become our greatest assets.... Still, Indigenous victories depend on mismatching universal rights and local cultural legacies, expert science and place-based knowledge, social justice, and communal precedence."[25] It is a view of the world that Tsing and others have characterized as "patchy."[26]

With multiplicity at its heart, this view does not generalize or dilute the countless, searing, individual understandings of indigeneity, and it is not Indigenous knowledge regarded as a mythic or monolithic target of yet more extraction or cloying white cultural cooptation. Instead, does this indigeneity begin to model another way of being on the earth even for those who have depraved and repulsive ancestors? Are these ways of being

for all those in a coalition of the impure who choose to confront their whiteness and turn to work at the edges of not one but many recovered centers of knowledge eclipsed by the last five hundred years of stupidity?

Maybe this discontinuous commons, together with "a particular inhabitation of earth" that is multivalent and "inconsistent," begins to claim special repertoires for activism that go beyond international or global solidarity to planetary solidarity. "Global" is often used in relation to modern, totalizing organizations that address governance beyond nations—dreams of a new world order as a singular platform parsed by an anointed philosophical, legal, or technical language. But, again countering the white/modern/Enlightenment mind reproduced in that conception, planetary solidarity might involve shared goals that are addressed with extremely particular and situated responses. If the global tends toward the universal, the planetary tends toward the mutual, the patchy, and the partial—the discontinuous world that cannot be parsed with an elementary particle, or, after the Zapatistas, "the world where many worlds fit."[27]

If dangers and abuses can be converted to extra powers, a shift to planetary solidarity meets an obvious opportunity to convert climate catastrophes—catastrophes harming those who are already the victims of what Robyn Maynard and Leanne Betasamosake Simpson call the "world-ending" logics of the last five hundred years.[28] Can worldmaking activism, aware of its planetary histories and futures, not only divert these additional world-ending forces of climate catastrophe away from the usual victims but also convert their power into new sovereignties and solidarities? This is a fight over land that is

over fifty miles thick and filled with gases and solids. Its atmospheres move in swirling fronts that disregard state boundaries or demarcations of property. It does not respond to geometry, and it cannot be enclosed. It seeps and fills volumetrically. It plays tricks that can enhance dissensus. With forms of lethality different from war, it creeps up from behind to slap you and swallow you with hot water or fire. It can be adjusted with remote effects from multiple positions within the diaspora—situated knowledge as well as a mobile exchange across oceans and continents.

But this fight can also deploy the superabundances associated with live organizations of mutualism and commoning on land that is not regarded as property. It is no wonder that Olúfémi O. Táíwò returns to the activism of the 1960s and '70s to inspire a planetary approach to reparations.[29] Physical, spatial consequences of atmospheric chemicals, together with the constantly self-replenishing resources of community economies, inundate the puny financial abstractions of capital. Now not only are the calculations of capital zeroing out in the face of floods and fires but community economies are also creating incalculable excessive values with the capacity to address the incalculable debt of reparations.

Palestine may be among the most potent, graphic examples of a discontinuous archipelago of commoning linked by a mobility commons. Mahdi Sabbagh writes about the 2021 demonstrations in Silwan that invoked sumud as a communal awareness holding ground within a contested state while also reaching out to a mobile diaspora.[30] Those who have not been isolated and surrounded as captives can only try to empathize, but, through that unspeakable pain, does Palestine model a special shared condition? Without relinquishing land that has become the contested territory of nations—thus rewarding those who long for war—does the collective fight for another kind of land provide it with extra powers?

Something seems so important about the shape of places that are at once situated and surrounded by hostility while also being diasporic and linked to allies. In a way that may seem counterintuitive, discontinuity, inconsistency, and patchiness are the secret weapons of their activism. They contribute to defiance and dissensus while reflecting a world of multiple ecologies that rely on difference and interdependence. To match a spectrum of dangers there is a spectrum of regenerative possibilities for being human. To match the situated and mobile forces of colonizing, capitalizing, and globalizing, there is a situated as well as a mobile commons with a capacity for planetary sovereignty and solidarity. These activists can put their bodies in specific places to stop political superbugs while also shape-shifting to become the moving targets that keep the superbugs starved and disoriented. It is not only a symmetrical war against the stupidity of the last five hundred years. It is the flowering of live organizations of community and kinship. It is a release into abundant, unstoppable, entangled economies to overwhelm that stupidity with potentials that are already there, if everyone tries to be in Palestine. ●

ENDNOTES

. "Sovereignty" in this discussion does not mean only a supreme force, but the apparatus that accompanies an entity's defendable right to exist.

2. For one such historical synthesis, see Robin D. G. Kelley, *Freedom Dreams: The Black Radical Imagination* (Boston: Beacon Press, 2002).

. Malcolm X with Alex Haley, *The Autobiography of Malcolm X* (New York: Grove Press, 1965).

4. Anne Garland Mahler, *From the Tricontinental to the Global South: Race, Radicalism, and Transnational Solidarity* (Durham, NC: Duke University Press, 2018). See also an archive of *TRIcontinenal* magazine: https://search. freedomarchives.org/; Josh MacPhee, "Constructing Third World Struggle: The Design of the OSPAAAL & Tricontinenal," *Funambulist* 22, March–April 2019): 50–55.

5. Cynthia Ann Young, *Soul Power Culture, Radicalism, and the Making of a U.S. Third World Left* (Durham NC: Duke University Press, 2006), 00–144.

5. Sophia Azeb, "Pan-African Performance and Possibility in North Africa: Lessons from Algiers 1969," *Funambulist* 32 November–December 2020): 28–33.

7. Derrick E. White, *The Challenge of Blackness: The Institute of the Black World and Political Activism of the 1970s* (Gainesville: University Press of Florida, 2011).

8. Robert F. Williams, *Negroes with Guns* (New York: Marzani and Munsell, 1962); Timothy B. Tyson, *Radio Free Dixie: Robert F. Williams and the Roots of Black Power* (Chapel Hill: University of North Carolina Press, 1999).

9. Kelley, *Freedom Dreams*; Edward Onaci, *Free the Land: The Republic of New Afrika and the Pursuit of a Black Nation-State* (Chapel Hill: University of North Carolina Press, 2020); Paul Karolczyk, "Subjugated Territory: The New Afrikan Independence Movement and the Space of Black Power" (dissertation, Louisiana State University, 2014); Dan Berger, "'Free the Land': Fifty Years of the Republic of New Afrika," *Black Perspectives*, April 10, 2018, https://www.aaihs.org/ free-the-land-fifty-years-of-the-republic-of-new-afrika/.

10. Vijay Prashad, *The Poorer Nations: A Possible History of the Global South* (New York: Verso, 2012); "The Challenge of the South: Report of the South Commission: Conclusions and Recommendations," *Foreign Trade Review* 25, no. 3 (1990): 293–316, https://doi. org/10.1177/0015732515 900307.

11. Prashad, *Poorer Nations*.

12. Adom Getachew, *Worldmaking after Empire: The Rise and Fall of Self-Determination* (Princeton: Princeton University Press, 2019).

13. Mahler, *From the Tricontinental*, 237.

14. See, for example, Denise Ferreira da Silva, *Toward a Global Idea of Race* (Minneapolis: University of Minnesota Press, 2007); Saidiya V. Hartman, *Wayward Lives, Beautiful Experiments: Intimate Stories of Upheaval* (New York: Norton, 2019); Tiffany Lethabo King, *The Black Shoals: Offshore Formations of Black and Native Studies* (Durham, NC: Duke University Press, 2019); and Katherine McKittrick, *Dear Science and Other Stories* (Durham, NC: Duke University Press, 2021).

15. David Scott, "The Re-Enchantment of Humanism: An Interview with Sylvia Wynter," *Small Axe* 8 (September 2000): 119–207.

16. Hanif Adurraqib and Fred Moten, "Building a Stairway to Get Us Closer to Something Beyond This Place," *Millennials Are Killing Capitalism,* May 13, 2021, https://millennialsarekillingcapitalism.libsyn.com/hanif-abdurraqib-fred-moten-building-a-stairway-to-get-us-closer-to-something-beyond-this-place; Stefano Harney and Fred Moten, *The Undercommons: Fugitive Planning and Black Study* (Minor Compositions, 2013), https://www.minorcompositions.info/wp-content/uploads/2013/04/undercommons-web.pdf.

17. Arturo Escobar, *Designs for the Pluriverse: Radical Interdependence, Autonomy, and the Making of Worlds* (Durham, NC: Duke University Press, 2018), 206–7, 281.

18. J. K. Gibson-Graham, Jenny Cameron, and Stephen Healy, *Take Back the Economy: An Ethical Guide for Transforming Our Communities* (Minneapolis: University of Minnesota Press, 2013).

19. Peter Linebaugh, *The Magna Carta Manifesto: Liberties and Commons for All* (Berkeley: University of California Press, 2008); Peter Linebaugh and Marcus Rediker, *The Many-Headed Hydra: Sailors, Slaves, Commoners, and the Hidden History of the Revolutionary Atlantic* (Boston: Beacon Press, 2013).

20. Mimi Sheller, *Mobility Justice: The Politics of Movement in an Age of Extremes* (New York: Verso, 2018), 159.

21. David Graeber and David Wengrow, *The Dawn of Everything: A New History of Humanity* (New York: Picador, 2021).

22. For one of these caveats, see Lana Tatour, "The Culturalisation of Indigeneity: The Palestinian-Bedouin of the Naqab and Indigenous Rights," *International Journal of Human Rights,* April 26, 2019, https://www.tandfonline.com/doi/full/10.1080/13642987.2019.1609454, accessed May 15, 2022.

23. Ahmad Amara and Yara Hawari, "Using Indigeneity in the Struggle for Palestinian Liberation," Alshabaka, August 8, 2019, https://al-shabaka.org/commentaries/using-indigeneity-in-the-struggle-for-palestinian-liberation/, accessed April 10, 2022; Steven Salaita, "American Indian Studies and Palestinian Solidarity: The Importance of Impetuous Definitions," *Decolonization: Indigeneity, Education & Society* 6, no. 1 (2017): 1–28; Brenna Bhandar, *Colonial Lives of Property: Law, Land, and Racial Regimes of Ownership* (Durham, NC: Duke University Press, 2018); Mark Rifkin, "Indigeneity, Apartheid, Palestine: On the Transit of Political Metaphors," *Cultural Critique* 95 (Winter 2017): 25–70.

24. Saidiya Hartman, Aisha K. Finch, Tiffany Lethabo King, and Kyle T. Mays, "Freedom and Fugitivity," June 11, 2021, Mellon Foundation Sawyer Seminar, UCLA Luskin Institute on Inequality and Democracy and Black Feminism Initiative at UCLA, https://vimeo.com/563066318.

25. Anna Tsing, "Indigenous Voice" in *Indigenous Experience Today,* ed. Marisol de la Cadena and Orin Starn (London: Routledge, 2007), 57.

26. Anna Lowenhaupt Tsing, Andrew S. Mathews, and Nils Bubandt, "Patchy Anthropocene: Landscape Structure, Multispecies History, and the Retooling of Anthropology," *Current Anthropology* 60, no. S20 (August 2019): 186–97.

27. Escobar, *Designs for the Pluriverse,* 17.

28. Robyn Maynard and Leanne Betasamosake Simpson, *Rehearsals for Living* (Chicago: Haymarket Books, 2022), 7.

29. Olúfẹ́mi O. Táíwò, *Reconsidering Reparations* (Oxford University Press, 2022).

30. Mahdi Sabbagh, "Sumud: Repertoires of Resistance in Silwan," *Public Culture* 34, no. 3 (2022): 495–514.

DINA OMAR

REFLECTIONS ON STRUCTURAL GASLIGHTING

The eyes said to the tongue
Go search for the words
That could say what I say
—Andalusian poem,
told by Andrés Segovia (Nupen, 1967)

In a lecture last spring, Palestinian artist Sliman Mansour said, "There are many conspiracies against the Palestinians. This is not paranoia, it is a basic feature of our lives." The statement was almost comforting to hear out loud because it confirmed a disquieting reality that I think about a great deal. How does fear of being dubbed a "conspiracy theorist" become enough to keep sane and sober voices quiet? How many of us stay quiet about the messy details of our collective oppression because

we know all too well how Palestinian words are subject to intense scrutiny, excerpting, and reframing in a manner that compounds a dynamic of abuse where Palestinians are at the receiving end of colonial violence and Israelis are placed at an advantage at seemingly every turn?

How does one gauge the difference between a healthy measure of suspicion and conspiratorial paranoia? What is the difference between accidentally slipping up, communicating, or doing the wrong thing and gaslighting? According to the literature, gaslighting is a conscious and intentionally crafted abuse tactic used to make victims question their reality. It is a form of intense manipulation where audiences are brought in to participate and prolong abuse. What are the linguistic and environmental clues that cause victims of gaslighting to question themselves and their reality?

How is gaslighting built into the infrastructure of the Israeli settler-colonial project?[1] While the environmental violence and physical infrastructure of the occupation are well documented, less studied are the indirect epistemic and symbolic violences that normalize colonial violence happening in real time. For example, ever wonder what editorial boards at the *New York Times* calibrate when characterizing internationally funded settlement projects that routinely dispossess Indigenous people as "new neighborhoods"? Who decides to see or not see violence, or who has the luxury of not seeing violence?

One design feature of long-term narcissistic abuse is a splitting between a domestic sphere rife with struggles of domination and control covered over by elaborate and extensive efforts made to promote an image of normalcy, altruism even, and the public sphere.[2] While the term "gaslighting" has gained notoriety in recent years, it remains under-theorized and used in ways that lack context and relationality to the controlling processes present in the commonplace. In this piece I am less concerned with trying to prove that the example I present is an instance of gaslighting in a psychological sense. Rather, I wish to focus on the effects of gaslighting in a sociological sense, what work it does in the world in terms of social relations.

For this piece I draw from an experience I had where language and violence felt, to me at that moment, one and the same. I wish to examine a nervous breakdown I experienced at an international forum that

markets itself as concerned with human rights while dramatically obfuscating and structurally contributing to a source of Palestinian oppression. I would also like to draw the reader's attention to the cues, sometimes subtle and sometimes overt, involved in scapegoating and blaming the victim. I want to examine the less visible aspects of violence as a multidimensional and imperfect analytic framework and the ways shame reemerges throughout.[3] Taking Gayatri Spivak's intervention as a point of departure, there is confoundingly little written about how epistemic and institutional violence shapes and is shaped by the neoliberal institutions we operate within.[4] In this case, I am concerned with how institutional norms that seem unrelated to key flashpoints happening in Palestine today compound how the brute colonial violence unfolding on the ground in real time is experienced.

In psychology, gaslighting is understood as an effect of a pathological interpersonal relationship, often with a family member or intimate partner, in which one person (the victim) is manipulated into doubting their sanity and sense of reality by someone else engaging in intimidating, manipulative, and aggressive behavior. The relationship between Israeli intelligence agencies, the Israel lobby, Israeli law, the Israeli military, and the normalization of surveillance of and violence against Palestinians, in real life and in representation, mirrors gaslighting as a key component of long-term narcissistic abuse.[5]

What does it mean when an ethnic cleansing is glossed over and abetted by the inertia of institutional norms? This question is not about mental health. What concerns me is a sociopolitical dynamic that implicates every person within the sphere of Israel's influence in its nation-building project. It is in this field where the economic logic of militarized violence plays out in the personal spaces and psyches of the targets and where Israeli psychological warfare mimics relationships of narcissistic abuse. It is my hope that saying these things out loud opens up space for considering what systemic gaslighting by Israeli intelligence and security experts, and its dependents and enablers, feels like through the eyes of its victims.

Drawing from literature in psychological anthropology and psychoanalysis, this piece seeks to advance a framework to better understand how profoundly disorienting structural gaslighting is, and to conceptualize gaslighting not merely as an effect of an abusive interpersonal relationship but as part of larger sociopolitical dynamics and, crucially, as part of worldmaking. By theorizing systemic gaslighting as something that can be built into social life and environments, it can then be identified, neutralized, and hopefully stripped of its power to suppress.

The Palestinian Authority Is a Subcontractor for Israeli Colonialism

Ironically enough, the example I want to discuss was at the Oslo Freedom Forum (OFF), a setting where the language of humanitarianism and the universality of human rights abounds. It was precisely what these slogans were covering up in relation to Palestine that triggered a nervous breakdown. The OFF is an annual conference funded by the Human Rights Foundation and other private foundations concerned with championing individual freedom against tyranny. The

official slogan of the OFF since its establishment in 2009 has been "Challenging Power." I am using the example of the OFF merely because it was one of the most recent and one of the more obvious examples of an institution that publicly poses as a promoter and protector of human rights, free speech, and freedom (religious, academic, political, etc.) but falls squarely in the neoliberal "progressive except for Palestine" camp.

I was invited to attend the 2022 Oslo Freedom Forum as one of my first assignments for a new consultancy job. It was supposed to be a launching pad to begin networking and building relationships. I attended the conference as both an enthusiastic participant and as a critical skeptic, two somewhat incompatible roles I am still trying to hold in productive tension. In discussing neoliberalism as a paradigm, I am not making claims that one person or thing is bad and evil or all good and altruistic altogether. Aside from the normative assessments that accompany such a hefty term, it is important for the purposes of this piece to identify neoliberalism as an overarching, inescapable socioeconomic paradigm that we're all living in.

With the exception of the World Economic Forum, few examples of the paradigmatic hypocrisies of neoliberalism are more glaring than at the OFF. Global policy prescriptions are presented as universal moral imperatives; indignation as well as the ability to grieve become selective. Palestine being arguably one of the most popular freedom movements in the world, in terms of sheer numbers and capacity to organize at the grassroots level, is, nevertheless, noticeably avoided and sidestepped at this "global gathering of activists." The selective outrage was the result of either human error and procedural issues or strategic omissions deliberately made to protect economic and security interests.

While the OFF has taken up the topic of Palestine in the past (how could they not?), it is clearly a taboo subject within the space. The OFF has hosted conversations on Palestine twice, once in 2013 and once at this conference in 2022 where I was in attendance. These sessions were promoted to be about Palestinian freedom. They were specifically limited to critiques against the Palestinian Authority (PA) and Hamas and not about freedom from the tyrannies of Israeli settler colonialism. It is important to examine this line between holding the Palestinian Authority accountable for its role in enabling Israeli settler-colonial violence and the tendency to scapegoat the PA as the primary culprit for the precarious and oppressive material conditions under which Palestinians live. I believe that it is important to do this transparently, even while running the risk of potentially getting some things wrong, because the role of the PA within the larger cosmology of ethnic cleansing is a mirror of a larger colonial condition where psychological warfare is embedded in the daily policing of people's lives—thus making the difference between mistakes and manipulation difficult to discern.

Israel was mentioned throughout the OFF; it was celebrated as a possible host for peace talks between Russia and Ukraine. Israel was casually brought up in a positive light for opening its hospitals to Ukrainians wounded by the Russian occupation. Israel was brought up for sharing technology with Ukrainian dissidents. Palestine was not brought up in this regard. Palestinian activists were not brought up.

In a 2009 article titled "The Horrors of Israeli Peace," the Palestinian social theorist and lawyer Samira Esmeir argues that discourse about peace functions to hide violence happening in plain sight. Esmeir suggests that the Palestinian Authority was formed, in theory, as the police force

tasked with protecting people by keeping the peace in majority-Palestinian areas that Israel chooses not to take over (yet).[6] Esmeir argues that, since the Oslo Accords were signed and the PA established, the PA has functioned as hired subcontractors that act as the first line of offense for Israeli occupiers. Many now call this "security coordination"—a special relationship between the Israeli military and the PA, which safeguards the occupation rather than protects people from state violence.[7] The security coordination relationship polices and monitors Palestinian criticism of the PA but primarily intends to thwart any and all resistance to the colonial occupation.

Critiques of the PA were circulated widely in the wake of two political murders in particular: that of Bassel al-Araj, who was murdered on March 6, 2017, in a shootout with Israeli occupation forces in coordination with the PA, and that of Nizar Banat, who was murdered on June 24, 2021, while in PA custody in Ramallah. The murders of al-Araj and Banat are by no means exceptional. Rather, they generated somewhat loud and far-reaching reactions because the two men were well-known intellectuals with deep and wide social networks. During the summer and fall of 2021, mass protests against the PA because of Banat's murder resulted in even more politically motivated arrests.

Challenges to the PA's legitimacy emerge regularly; their credibility is seemingly never not called into question. These critiques are delivered in decisive and fierce lectures, in nuanced and smart analyses such as those of Alaa Tartir at al-Shabaka, in demands to restructure and expedite elections for the Palestinian Legislative Council (PLC), in reports written by the UN, in protests and grassroots movement work such as *Tal3at* (طالعات), organized by women for women to make life more livable in Palestine. Some propose gradual reform; others call for a total overhaul of the PA. Such criticisms are often made despite the threat of great consequences. For example, in June 2021, the PA physically and psychologically assaulted and harassed women protesters, proceeded to confiscate their phones, and attempted to use photos and material on their phones to entrap them. These examples and the textured analysis they require were left absent and thus unexamined at the OFF.

In all the above-mentioned examples, criticizing and calling into question the legitimacy of the PA is appropriate, productive, and even imperative. These instances incorporate context, they respond to specific infringements, are historically grounded, and offer systemic analysis. In the most astute criticisms of the PA, one can recognize, in language and spirit, at the core, the overarching goal of Palestinian liberation in mind.[8]

Something Seemed Off

Again, the session on Palestine at the OFF in 2022 was the only session dedicated to Palestine since 2013. Ironically, the session was titled "The Future of Palestine," and every seat in the room was filled. There were a sizable number of people standing up because no extra seats were available. The overwhelming interest is a phenomenon in line with other experiences I had in settings where the topic of Palestine is considered taboo—interest is high, and people show up. Shortly after celebrated journalist Shireen Abu Akleh was murdered, a quote of hers circulated online: "In some absences the presence is greater."

The fact that Fadi Elsalameen was the only speaker to represent Palestine at a forum like the OFF is, in and of itself, part of a larger structural problem. The moderator for this session introduced the speaker and described him as someone who works for a DC-based think tank, specializes in national security, and believes bitcoin is a way for Palestinians to fight PA corruption. They also mentioned that he has one million followers on Facebook. Literally anyone who does not represent the "national security interests" of the US and Israeli war economies would have been a better option as a speaker.

Things that cosmetically seemed like gestures of solidarity were selectively curated and delivered in a way that felt slightly off. Elsalameen began his talk with a moment of silence for Shireen Abu Akleh. He likely mentioned Abu Akleh because I

and others at the conference implored him to do so, after a previous panel dedicated to protecting journalists and freedom of speech had not mentioned her even though she had been shot dead by Israeli military officers ten days before the conference began. In setting up the moment of silence, Elsalameen said that Abu Akleh was "killed in crossfire in Jenin Camp." He chose not to describe Abu Akleh's murder as part of a repeated pattern of targeted killings and attempts to silence journalists. His omitting of Israeli culpability was the first glimpse into the overall tone of the session.

Elsalameen's central theme was "PA corruption." It felt like the purpose was to embarrass and shame the PA. These criticisms were not carefully reflexive, in the manner of the critiques mentioned above, nor were they programmatic attempts to replace the governing body with a represen-tative and democratic one. Rather, aspects of Elsalameen's talk emphasized that the Palestinians have failed to form a func-tioning government and that government corruption is a result of nepotism, as if the Palestinians themselves are responsible for their own suffering. This angle emphasizes shame and points it toward the victims. Shame is debilitating in that it convinces the victim that they are victimized or at a disadvantage because of something they did, that there is something wrong with them.

Not mentioning Israeli culpability as the main agent responsible for steering and engendering PA corruption was the loudest aspect of Elsalameen's presentation. It seemed like Elsalameen had a set of objectives he needed to externalize for some sort of public record: PA officials are corrupt "tyrants." The PA is responsible for the suffering of the Palestinians, for suppressing free speech; it "fails to protect journalists" and "targets people for expressing their opinions online." The PA holds the Palestinians hostage and uses them as "human shields."

These points are not merely typical neoliberal ideas about corruption, sprinkled with racist undertones ("the corrupt Arab") that one expects. Rather, these points seemed to be taken out of the Israeli ministry of strategic affairs handbook. In a discussion titled "The Future of Palestine," why not take the opportunity to discuss the themes and subjects highlighted in this anthology, which looks to Palestinian futurity with hope and aspirations for freedom? Why not focus on Palestinian methodologies in forming and sustaining Palestinian cultural and intellectual continuity traditions, and, crucially, modes of refusal? Indeed, any serious reflection on contemporary Palestinian history will point to Palestinian futures as vibrant in their potential resistance and as possibly providing a blueprint for how to live a meaningful life in a world of "everywhere war." The Palestinian story is filled with dispossession, psychological warfare, scapegoating, and gaslighting that often pass as "expertise" inside the halls of power, the academy, and beyond. And while war may be a reality everywhere that is by no means exceptional to the Palestinian experience, as the reality of war encroaches on the lives of more and more people globally, paying attention to Palestine is important for understanding the processes and contradictions at the center of the US and Israeli war economies and how to thrive in conditions that feel and sometimes are postapocalyptic. Looking at Palestinian material and cultural

production provides insights for how to design counterhegemonic expression, analysis, and space.[9]

Consider the awesome and unfolding mobilization efforts such as: #savesheikhjarrah, #savemasaferyatta, #savesilwan, #gazaunderattack, responses to the murder of Shireen Abu Akleh, Indigenous resistance efforts against land theft in Beita and Aqrabah and the impending demolition of historic homes in Lifta, the dispossession of dozens of families in al-Wadi al-Ahmar and the bulldozing of Palestinian farmlands throughout the Naqab. The ethnic cleansing of Palestine is a project happening now, in real time, before our eyes. Reframing this ethnic cleansing as history, a conflict, a confusing stalemate, an inevitability, a Jewish homecoming, a War on Terror, a beacon of technological advancement, and Arab refusal to engage are rebranding attempts, crucial to the ethnic cleansing project itself.

The massive popular support for Palestinian freedom, as well as the influence of those who advocate for it and their importance to freedom struggles globally, cannot be overstated. The silence regarding such movements in a forum like OFF that supposedly challenges power is deafening. The summer of 2020, which saw an acceleration of settler violence and expansion in the West Bank; acute, eliminatory violence in Gaza, with entire families murdered in Israeli bombing campaigns; and land stealing in the Naqab, saw protests for Palestinian freedom organized around the world. While Palestinian families are at present being expelled to make way for Israeli settlers, there are countless expressions of protest and refusal, from prisoner hunger strikes and direct action protests globally, to paintings, performance art, and writing. Undeniably the summer of 2020 illustrated that the subject of Palestinian freedom from Israeli colonialism is now present in Silicon Valley boardrooms and in activist meetings in Hong Kong. Beginning in May 2020, the Palestinian Youth Movement was part of organizing protests happening around the world. I attended three protests: one in Los Angeles with about 8,000 people, one in San Diego with about 3,000 people, and one in San Bernardino with about 500 people. There were smaller protests in other cities in Southern California like Anaheim, Redlands, and Lancaster. There were protests in the tens of thousands in London, Paris, Bogotá, Sydney, Rabat, Johannesburg. Cities like Chicago had between 2,000 and 3,000 people show up on different days in different parts of the city, from Bridgeview to the loop. The point is that there were protests in suburbs and smaller cities across the entire world.

In light of all this, Elsalameen's omissions become part of a larger geopolitical project—one that renders investing in infrastructure that makes the project of Israeli settler colonialism inevitable while maintaining that it is right and good to not invest in Palestine or her people. Indeed, it seemed like the effect, and perhaps the purpose, of Elsalameen's talking points was to mark Palestinians as unfundable and to sow doubt and confusion about the source of their unfreedom. In a forum where justice activists and peace-makers are supposed to interface with donors interested in supporting righteous causes

against tyranny and for peace, focusing on the PA in this manner seemed to represent a deliberate effort to minimize questions about Israel's role in allowing, protracting, and intensifying Palestinian dispossession, death, and suffering. By focusing on the PA's shortcomings and corruption, with no mention of Palestinian resilience, ingenuity, and deep connections to the land and each other, or the mobilization efforts against both Israeli colonialism and the PA, the speaker signaled an attempt to blame the victim and diminish their achievements while pretending that their suffering and grief happened as a result of their own doing and their culture, and within a vacuum.

Rhetorically Elsalameen's presentation was similar to referring to "Black on Black" crime in contexts of police killings of unarmed Black civilians or saying a woman was "asking for it" because "look at how she was dressed," in contexts of rape. Psychologist and scholar Jennifer J. Freyd describes these rhetorical shorthands as "DARVO" behavior: "Deny, Attack, and Reverse Victim and Offender."[10] Again, a key feature of long-term intimate partner abuse, and a key component of psychological warfare, is the element of reputation management. Perpetrators denying any and all wrongdoing, then claiming the position of victim, is a well-studied strategy of the Israeli government, used to "neutralize" the effects of testimonies from victims.[11]

Traversing the Gap
I snapped. A scream emerged from some place inside me, "*Ikhras*!!!" I've never screamed so loud before in my life. It felt like some external yet familiar force briefly took up residence in me. I felt possessed;

44

something was communicating through me. I ran out yelling, "Shut up, shut up! I can't listen anymore! You are a liar! Get me out of here! I want to go home! Get me out of here!"

I am a bit embarrassed about it, weeks after the fact. Viscerally, I feel embarrassed. However, when I think about it intellectually, I don't regret it. It felt like I was a channel, expressing a force that I cannot explain, not a rational person performing a professional role. In venues like the OFF you hear slogans that, in other contexts, can stir a fire inside your body. However, when they are said on a stage like that of the OFF it sounds as ordinary as a watered-down version of a Folgers Coffee advertisement from the 1990s. And for me to not be paralyzed by the embarrassment I need to suspend preconceived standards of professionalism; at this point nothing feels closer to home for me as a Palestinian than tiptoeing around the facts in hopes not to be flagged by the arbitrators on the use of hegemonic violence. That said, I am also aware that there are times when one, or many, veer too far into the direction of chaos and lack of decorum, and for that reason alone I don't wish to glorify and celebrate breaking open like that.

One of the slogans we heard recycled during the OFF was "Freedom Is Not Free." To be fair, it is a compelling mantra that was mostly applied to efforts to raise money to support Ukrainian resistance against the Russian military occupation. The irony, not lost on me, is that the point of the OFF is to court funders to support human rights defenders. The invocation that freedom is not free is something serious, it is concrete, it is an appeal for resources.

Palestinians witness firsthand the heavy cost that too many continue to pay with what little they have for the possibility of freedom. Indeed, some pay and pay and pay, with their land, with their homes, with their lives, with their time, with the distances they are forced to traverse to be together, with threats against their loved ones, with loss of money, with quite literally their taxes, with the lifelines and support systems cut, with the lines of communication cut, with their culture and livelihoods constantly and stunningly created only to be looted, stolen, and repackaged for the benefit of their oppressors, with land and memories stolen, experiences negated or denied, bodies violated, and families broken apart. Palestinians are the target of Israel's narcissistic petulance and abuse, and everywhere is indeed violence—psychological, epistemic, structural, and financial. Palestinians live abbreviated lives and there is so much bellowing beneath the surface of our decisions and imposed silence. That is what I was seeing all around me at the OFF: well-dressed and well-meaning people nodding and listening intently at a meticulously orchestrated event that was unfolding exactly as planned. My scream was just one small interjection to "spoil the pretty picture."[12]

With regard to Palestine, words matter exponentially; the frameworks that echo in the hallways of prestigious institutions are often designed specifically to separate us from our own thoughts, our memories, each other, and ourselves. One of the most valuable lessons of recent Palestinian history is the renewed critical engagement with the use of language. When we do not agree with the criteria or framework, when the words used to describe who we are create conflict in us, it is imperative not to allow deliberately coercing records to stand unabated. Ghassan Kanafani insisted on challenging tacit assumptions embedded in colonial logics. Direct reframing remains one of the most effective Palestinian methods and modes of representation, survival, and refusal, which has been extended through today by activists like Mohammed and Muna el-Kurd.

I did not realize it then, but the scream was my body "rejecting that abstraction, that enormity"[13] and conjuring a sound, which can also be expressed through writing reflections like this, through art, and organizing efforts, all of which can and do work as a particular kind of agency that remediates this gap, unburdening oneself from feelings of isolation and shame. The screaming was indicative of a failure of language, but it opened space for the generation of new language, allowing the audience to critically respond to shape this new language, this reflection notwithstanding.

There is a chasm between the inescapable presence of Palestine in the lives of those who belong to her and Palestine's illegibility in the institutions that Palestinians run and operate within. This chasm mirrors contemporary debates in social theory between meaning and materiality. Incorporating the analytic frameworks that help us understand routinized, latent, and epistemic violence also helps us understand this chasm.

The chasm is also one that separates risks and rewards between those writing and speaking in ways that objectify, shame, and demean those written and spoken about, between those photographed and those taking the picture. Looking to contemporary Palestinian resistance efforts, such as direct action, organizing, and cultural production that intervenes as a reconfiguration of that gaze where Palestinians invest and conduct themselves based on their reality, on their own terms, is potentially instructive and liberating. In this real-time moment of refutation, a particular kind of agency is revealed, one that traverses and remediates the gap between what the eyes see and what words the tongue can say. ◆

ENDNOTES

1. The term "gaslighting" comes from the play written by Patrick Hamilton (1938) and adapted to film by George Cukor (1944) starring Charles Boyer (playing Gregory) and Ingrid Bergman (playing Paula). The male protagonist, Gregory, convinces the neighborhood community that his wife, Paula, is unhinged and unwell to deflect and cover up that he murdered Paula's aunt years prior, is still looking to steal jewels that belonged to Paula's aunt, and is trying to steal the home Paula inherited from her aunt. Gregory "slowly and systematically" tries to convince Paula to act against her instincts. In so doing, Gregory portrays himself publicly to the neighborhood community as a patient and gentle caretaker.

2. Paige L. Sweet, "The Sociology of Gaslighting," *American Sociological Review* 84, no. 5 (2019): 851–75?

3. A central feature of narcissistic abuse is the denial of one's reality. The origin in terms of causation is unclear, as the denial is imposed by the abuser as a form of reputation management as well as self-imposed as a survival mechanism in the form of internal minimizing and self-invalidating ruminations and feelings of shame. Feelings of "How could I allow this to happen to me?" are often precursors to unprocessed shame.

4. Gayatri Chakravorty Spivak, "Can the Subaltern Speak?" in *Colonial Discourse and Post-Colonial Theory*, ed. Patrick Williams and Laura Chrisman (London: Routledge, 2015), 66–111.

5. Joan Lachkar, "Paradox of Peace: Folie a Deux in Marital and Political Relationships," *Journal of Psychohistory* 22, no. 2 (1994): 199.

6. Samira Esmeir, "The Horrors of Israel's Peace," *Middle East Report Online*, January 22, 2009, https://merip.org/2009/01/the-horrors-of-israels-peace/.

7. Alaa Tartir, "The Palestinian Authority Security Forces: Whose Security?" Al-Shabaka, May 16, 2017, https://al-shabaka.org/briefs/palestinian-authority-security-forces-whose-security/.

8. Rana Barakat, Mouin Rabbani, Dina Omar, Fajr Harb, Hani al-Masri, As'ad Ghanem, Yassmine Hamayel, and Aziza Khalidi, "An Open Debate on Palestinian Representation," Al-Shabaka, May 1, 2013, https://al-shabaka.org/roundtables/open-debate-palestinian-representation/.

9. Nadera Shalhoub-Kevorkian, "Counter-Narratives of Palestinian Women: The Construction of Her-story and the Politics of Fear," in *Gender and Violence in the Middle East*, ed. Moha Ennaji and Fatima Sadiqi (London: Routledge, 2011), 47–77.

10. Sarah Harsey and Jennifer J. Freyd, "Deny, Attack, and Reverse Victim and Offender (DARVO): What Is the Influence on Perceived Perpetrator and Victim Credibility?" *Journal of Aggression, Maltreatment & Trauma* 29, no. 8 (2020): 897–916.

11. Efrat Shoham, "Victim Rhetoric Among Sex Offenders: A Case Study of the Former Israeli President," *Journal of Politics and Law* 8, no. 1 (2015): 26.

12. June Jordan, "Poem on a New Year's Eve," *Directed by Desire: The Collected Poems of June Jordan* (Copper Canyon Press, 2007), 202–3.

13. Jordan, "Poem on a New Year's Eve."

TAREQ BACONI

WRETCHED GAZA: CONFRONTING THE ABJECT

What is abject . . . *is radically excluded and draws me toward the place where meaning collapses. . . . And yet, from its place of banishment, the abject does not cease challenging its master. . . . On the edge of non-existence and hallucination, of a reality that, if I acknowledge it, annihilates me. There, abject and abjection are my safe-guards. The primers of my culture.*
—Julia Kristeva, *Powers of Horror: An Essay on Abjection.*

We each carry within us a degree of self-loathing. A true self that is, knowingly or otherwise, hidden from the world in shame. In fear, also, that it might elicit judgment, or disrupt the norms around us that we are socialized into and come to abide by. Within every Self, there is an Other that is trampled on, marginalized, and suppressed in the anxious belief that its acknowledgment might destabilize the Self and bring it to ruin. That is to say, we are all, on some intimate level, familiar with abjection, with the wretchedness we feel at confronting the Other within or around us. The abject being, of course, all that is disgusting, repulsive, ugly, unfit to be in proper society, exceptional, subhuman.

Gaza is the abject of our time. It is a miserable stretch of land, overpopulated and dirty, drowning in its own shit and decrepit infrastructure, beaten and abused, on the brink of death refusing the dignity of passing, of letting go. In the Israeli collective psyche (but not just), Gaza is a dark place, full of terrorists, of angry hordes, a place where—in the words of a minister of justice no less—Palestinian mothers give birth to snakes, not babies.[1] Gaza is a nuisance that persistently clings to Israel, demanding attention, disrupting the lives of Israelis, seeking recognition. None will be forthcoming because deep within, in some shrouded corner, is a resounding truth that can never be fully banished even as it remains unspoken: The Gaza Strip is Israel's creation. In its present abject manifestation, Gaza is a colonial construct, territorially and demographically engineered to enable the emergence of a Zionist entity in Palestine.

For Gaza is a microcosm of Palestine.[2] Most of its inhabitants were ethnically cleansed from their nearby homes in Lydd, Jaffa, Bir Saba', Falouja, Jabalia, and other villages and towns in southern Palestine and beyond. Their confinement, and the settlement of the territories surrounding the strip with Jewish-only communities, are the logical endpoint of Zionist settler colonialism. From the early days of their movement at the turn of the last century, in a historical milieu where the great powers were steeped in colonialist thinking, Zionists have looked to Palestine as a homeland for the world's Jewish population, a geography that can pave the way for their self-determination. The natives of the land were either irrelevant in this thinking or placated as people who, with no political aspirations of their own, would welcome the imposition of European

modernity. Systems of territorial consolidation and demographic engineering followed, and arranged into a regime of apartheid with Israel's creation in 1948.

Building in rubble,
photo by author, 2015

What came about is a system, also, from which Palestinians were made abject. Gaza is the blueprint of how settler colonies build ostensible democracies—that is, democracies that are rooted in and emerge from apartheid—in this instance, a democracy solely for Jews that presides over a population of non-Jews. For Israel, such facts cannot be denied, nor can they be acknowledged, without the disintegration of

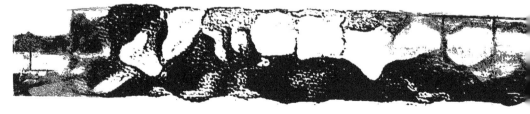

an intricately constructed myth. This is what the abject does; it demands a fundamental reformulation of the Self. It is a revolutionary demand that requires structural transformation for it to be accommodated. There can be no confrontation of what Gaza is, from an Israeli perspective, without a parallel concession that Zionist settler colonialism needs to come wholly undone for actual democracy to prevail. Hence, the power of the abject to annihilate.

Ostensible democracies that form the bedrock of contemporary Western civilization—be they French, American, or British—are rooted in histories of apartheid, slavery, and colonialism, and in presents of exploitative and racialized capitalism. American democracy, for instance, is rooted in white supremacy domestically and imperial violence globally. Countries that proclaim Western civilizational values at home elide the unwanted populations they have brutalized in pursuit of their superiority. There is a Gaza—an unwanted and dominated population—behind most stories of democratic rule, which is why the truth that Gaza embodies has the potential to dismantle our world order. It is no coincidence that Gaza has become a stand-in, a shorthand, for the major travails that plague our times, be they refugees, barricaded populations, overpopulation, police and military brutality, or ecological disasters.

The success of hegemony is predicated on dehumanization, and the role Gaza plays in the Israeli psyche is exactly the role other unwanted and undesirable communities play in the popular imagination of the powerful. It is a mirror unto the Self, and through its very existence, Gaza showcases state-of-the-art ways the powers of our time can deploy for dealing with that unwanted reflection. Confinement, surveillance, mass torture, de-development, de-ecologizing, imprisonment, starvation, bombardment; through such tactics and others, Gaza offers a road map for confronting and managing populations that must be forgotten so that the civilized of the world can claim their humanity and superiority.

Building in rubble,
photo by author, 2015

Palestinians in Gaza joke, morbidly, about their welcoming of a quick death from an F16 spewing fire over the slow suffocation of the blockade. They understand that the strangulation they live with, day in and day out, is the intended purpose—not their ultimate death. For the very unsustainability of Gaza, highlighted intermittently as if some urgent endpoint needs to be avoided, is precisely what sustains it: unsustainability in this instance is a structure, a process with its own logic, persisting in perpetuity.

51

Unsustainability is what allows the oppressors to pacify while also claiming a civilized status. Unsustainability, then, is a structure that can, and is, being replicated elsewhere.

Photo by author, 2015

Gaza is a prototype for stemming the flow of asylum seekers through the Mediterranean. Their containment in internment camps, whether in France or Libya, is an amateurish replica compared to the isolation and immobility Israel imposes on Gaza's inhabitants.[3] Structurally, Gaza resembles America's prison-industrial complex, which primarily incarcerates America's unwanted Black populations, as well as China's internment of Uighurs. Temporally, Gaza can be historically compared to apartheid South Africa's Bantustans and futuristically to the West Bank's Area A. Technologically, Gaza elaborates how mass surveillance, artificial intelligence, and spy software can immobilize, pacify, torture, and break populations.

Having been firmly conceptualized as the abject by its oppressors, it is no coincidence that Gaza is also burdened with the corollary of inspiration for those oppressed, in terms of Palestinian steadfastness and sumud.[4] From the early days of Israel's creation, Palestinians in Gaza have consistently attempted to return to their homes. From this strip, the leading *fedayeen* were birthed and politicized in the late 1940s, the PLO executive committee was formed in 1964, the first Intifada erupted in 1987, and Hamas emerged, officially, a year later. In popular parlance, Gaza is known as *umm al-muqawamma*, mother of resistance, affirming feminist revolutionary power in the struggle for justice. Gamal Abdel Nasser invited Che Guevara in 1959 and Jawaharlal Nehru in 1960 to visit the Gaza Strip, to showcase the power of this piece of land to mobilize the anticolonial movements of the Global South.[5]

This is precisely why Zionism has expended much effort and endless maneuverings to pacify the strip, most recently through the use of live sniper fire to kill and maim Palestinian protesters in the Great March of Return.[6] This has built on decades of drip-feeding Gaza's economy and controlling the flow of goods, down to the caloric value of food items, to ensure Palestinians there are maintained just above the level of official starvation, and managing the passage of people in and out, like cattle into a pen. From extrajudicial assassinations to economic pacification, from bombardment to occupation, and twelve full-fledged wars since 1948,[7] the Zionist regime has over-extended itself to break this strip of land. To no avail. The abject is persistent, ever-present, unerasable. And for colonial thinking and

52

rationale, the construction of the abject is central. Gaza exists as an abject not only because Israel has failed to eliminate it, but because Israel as a collective needs an abject to sustain itself. Through and against its very survival, Israel has fashioned itself as an Other that is better, more refined, that values life rather than death, unlike the wretched inhabitants of Gaza. Israel and Gaza exist in a dialectic whereby the existence of the Israeli collective is predicated on the abjection of Palestinians generally, and Gaza to a particular extreme.

It follows from this logic that Gaza will have a disproportionate role to play in the future liberation of Palestine. What a burden to place on the abject. Already denied, fatigued, humiliated, dismissed, taken to and kept on the brink of death, the abject is then called upon to liberate. A burden made more immense because, it must be said, Zionism is not a standalone ideology. As a settler-colonial movement, Zionism emerged alongside other colonial movements, and persists today by the continued support of the world's most affluent and powerful settler colony—the United States. The structures of oppression spanning our globe, institutionalizing racialized capitalism and colonialist inequalities, are interconnected and interdependent. Gaza might be immedi-

ately confronting Zionism, but understanding its abjection helps us grapple with the mechanics of oppression and degradation elsewhere. In that sense, while Gaza is the laboratory for the powerful, seeking to subjugate and hone their skills of oppression, it is also the laboratory for emancipation, for resistance, for asymmetric warfare.

Photo by author, 2015

As Fanon said, resistance to colonialism generates comprehensive creativity.[8] The word that comes to mind when thinking of Gaza and resistance is "innovation." Basic, almost childish tactics created in Gaza make regimes tremble. Balloons flying over fences leave colonizers shaking in their shelters. Kites lit aflame are met with a nuclear

power citing the need for self-defense. Condoms filled with flammable liquids leave settlers frozen in their tracks or cowering on the sides of the road. Smoke from flaming tires make snipers helpless and ineffective. Tunnels dug up in various sizes and lengths undermine a sophisticated machinery of border construction. This is what asymmetric warfare is. This is what Gaza teaches us.

The Mediterranean Sea, Gaza,
photo by author, 2015

As philosopher Julia Kristeva asserted, "In abjection, revolt is completely within being. . . . The subject of abjection is eminently productive of culture."[9] And productive Gaza is. The Great March of Return, which began in Gaza in 2018, is one of the longest sustained mass mobilizations in history and through its eruption reaffirmed the centrality of the right of return to the Palestinian struggle for liberation at precisely the time that our so-called leaders had, worn down and fatigued, acquiesced to pittances.

Structures of oppression are daunting, monolithic, seemingly immovable, and Palestinians often look at the Zionist regime as invincible. This, after all, is what made our self-appointed leaders accept partition and embrace the Oslo Accords, the very bedrock of apartheid, as a concession of their defeat.[10] How can this thriving Israeli powerhouse be forced to confront its original sin? But we have learned better. The latest Arab revolutions, for one, yielded an important lesson: the house of cards tumbles much more quickly than any young person in the region might have ever imagined. So quick, in fact, that it caught the revolutionaries unprepared, having focused the entirety of their effort on the long haul of bringing the dictator down, having failed to properly contend, also, with the possibility of their success. What do we do with this lesson as we see the counterrevolution fortify itself, with expanding interdependencies between the region's authoritarian regimes and its settler colonies emerging from the shadowy realm of clandestine relations? How do we take that lesson back to Gaza, specifically, and to Palestine more broadly, to further fortify their already ingenious resistance tactics? Cracks in the apartheid regime are showing—minor, to be sure, but visible—particularly after the Unity Intifada that unified Palestinians in an uprising from the river to the sea, and throughout the diaspora, in May 2021.[11] What must be done to push these cracks wide open? How can Gaza's liberation tactics, far from being isolated through the blockade, learn from and inspire the revolutionary tactics of the region?

And how do we take this lesson to other struggles shaping our world? The climate justice movement is similarly facing a daunting adversary, where the fossil fuel industry and the world's leading powers pay lip service to change while remaining enslaved by their inertia. Black Lives Matter faces institutionalized white supremacy that, despite the gains of the movement in 2019–2020, still holds on to anti-Blackness.

These struggles might appear distinct; they are anything but. Abjection has been forced, in different ways, onto myriad communities: Blacks, Arabs, Indigenous peoples, queers, Roma, women. A hierarchy of suffering has prevailed and has forced an acquiescence to subjugation. This is perhaps the most important lesson that Gaza can teach us. Just like the abject has the power to annihilate our oppressors, it can also break our spirits, unless we embrace our abjection fully and radically. Such an embrace of our mutual marginalization, each with its own history and context, creates networks of solidarity that are fluid, decentralized, and rooted in shared values of emancipation and liberation and shared learning, networks that are powerful and grounded.

Late journalist Samir Kassir, before he was assassinated, wrote of the Arab malaise that plagues the peoples of the region. He wrote of apathy, indifference, and lack of hope. There is a stuckness that is slowly choking all of us. How can it not? After that glimmer of light from the Arab revolutions a decade ago, we have now descended into a darkness that leaves us yearning for what came before. Our elders who advocated against disruption, saying things like *We have to be ruled by a strong man* and *We are not worthy of democracy* are vindicated. We have no reason to overcome our malaise.

Scenes from Gaza, photo by author, 2015

The most effective weapon our colonizers wield over us is to make us believe, on some fundamental level, that we are not worthy of better, of freedom and liberation, breaking our agency and forcing us to internalize our subjugation without even knowing that we have. Our oppressors have succeeded when we, in the corners of our hearts, truly believe that we are, after all, abject, the dregs of humanity, unworthy. We might not realize that we are doing so, choosing to believe instead the lies we are constructing about our modernity, progress, and stability—showcased in extravagant wealth and neoliberalism. But underneath the glitzy facade, the malaise persists.

Nayrouz Qarmout, a writer from Gaza, wrote a short story about a young, veiled girl on a visit to the beach in Gaza.[12] Called into the water by the beauty of the sun reflecting off the waves, the girl ventures away from her family and into the depths, deeper than she should have gone. Her veils weigh heavily on her and threaten to pull her down.

Cloaks that she had not quite asked for, that were hung on her body for her virtue and protection, turn deadly. The girl is rescued from drowning at the last minute by a young boy, a childhood crush, with an illicit bodily contact that she fears the patriarchal society around her will judge her for, even in the throes of death. She is horrified, also, because as she finally makes it out of the near-death experience, the fabrics of her wet clothes cling to her body, revealing more than they cover.

The clothes that we wear, the way we fashion ourselves, might be the essence of what is bringing us down. And in shedding them, there is shame. The alternative, however, is to drown in black waters. Shedding our clothes means removing the layers we have wrapped around our bodies to cover up ugly truths. Confronting our abjection means coming to terms with the very real, fear-driven factors that result in our malaise: patriarchy, anti-Blackness, corruption, nationalist fervor. We must confront all those things and many others. But we must also do more. We must fundamentally believe in victory and be willing to commit wholly to the long fight for its realization. Seeing Gaza as defeated, incapable, hamstrung, breaks our spirits. Seeing Palestinians as victims, as a dispersed people, as disposable bodies, confines us to the margins of history. The

truth, in contrast, is that the site of abjection is precisely the place of life, of alternatives, of political imagination. Out of the queerest of spaces, the ugliest of beings, the most extreme forms of abjection, beauty and revolution abound. Rather than succumbing to abjection, we must reclaim it. Instead of the abject annihilating us, it can transform us, help us overcome our learned helplessness.

This is what Gaza teaches us, every day, with every balloon and kite: our weakness is a site of innovation. From our abjection we have the capacity to disrupt and ultimately destroy structures of oppression, as a precursor to rebuilding more just futures. Gaza is intimately familiar to other marginalized peoples and communities elsewhere. It is known on an intrinsic level, understood, even under the layers of misrepresentation imposed on it by dominant narratives. That truth, if harnessed, has transformative potential,

even beyond the narrow confines of Palestine. There is solidarity among the abject—a collective interdependency that is as strong, as powerful, as that of the oppressors. Gaza, taken to the brink, still struggles, because it understands: the choice is not between life and death, the choice is between a life of freedom or a slow strangulation. With every balloon and every kite, it teaches us that our weakness can become our greatest strength.

What I am seeking to convey is the potential of radical honesty, a journey as collective as it is individual. In *Gaza as Metaphor,* the writer Selma Dabbagh writes, "There is a Gaza in all of us."[13] What would it mean for us to confront our abjection honestly? To overcome our fears and succumb to that internal voice of self-loathing that speaks of our possible defeat, of the errors we have acquiesced to out of fear or pride? Abjection is the primer of our culture. We

have, each of us, the potential to transform
out of our paralysis and into an activated
and innovative being. We can all, individually, contribute to a politics of liberation
that can sustain our movement, and speak
beyond it, arriving at a revolutionary politics
that is rooted in our present abjection and
that uses this position as a launching pad
from which to bring down the immovable.
Can a Palestinian war of liberation, which
is rooted in a specific historical and political
context, also exist as a lightning rod of radical empathy, one that can encompass other
struggles? Can this most confined of locales
act as an anchor to a sprawling ideology of
liberation and resistance, of fundamental
emancipation, of radical humanism, that
spans the globe?

For our colonizers, confronting the
abject entails a journey of deconstruction,
one that is violent and disruptive. For us,
Palestinians and allies seeking justice,
confronting our abjection as a source of
strength entails its own transformation,
one that is ultimately cathartic. There is no
choice otherwise. ●

ENDNOTES

1. Ishaan Tharoor, "Israel's New Justice Minister Considers All Palestinians to Be 'the Enemy,'" *Washington Post*, May 7, 2015, https://www.washingtonpost.com/news/worldviews/wp/2015/05/07/israels-new-justice-minister-considers-all-palestinians-to-be-the-enemy/.

2. Tareq Baconi, "Gaza and the One-State Reality," *Journal of Palestine Studies* 50, no. 1 (2021): 77–90, https://doi.org/10.1080/0377919X.2020.1842002.

3. Ian Urbina, "The Secretive Prisons That Keep Migrants Out of Europe," *New Yorker*, November 28, 2021, https://www.newyorker.com/magazine/2021/12/06/the-secretive-libyan-prisons-that-keep-migrants-out-of-europe.

4. See Mahdi Sabbagh, "Renewing Solidarity" in this volume.

5. Salman Abu Sitta, "Gaza Strip: The Lessons of History," *Gaza as Metaphor*, ed. Helga Tawil Souri and Dina Mattar (London: Hurst, 2016), 109.

6. B'Tselem, "On Unlawful Gunfire against Protesters in the Return Marches in Gaza," *B'Tselem*, October 28, 2021, https://www.btselem.org/gaza_strip/2018_unlawful_gunfire_against_protesters_in_return_marches.

7. Jean Pierre Filiu, *Gaza: A History* (Oxford: Oxford University Press, 2014).

8. Atef Alshaer, "In the Company of Frantz Fanon: The Israeli Wars and the National Culture of Gaza," *Gaza as Metaphor*, 149.

9. Julia Kristeva, *Powers of Horror: An Essay on Abjection* (New York: Columbia University Press, 1982), 45.

10. Tareq Baconi, "What Apartheid Means for Israel," *New York Review of Books*, November 5, 2021, https://www.nybooks.com/online/2021/11/05/what-apartheid-means-for-israel/.

11. Yara Hawari, "Defying Fragmentation and the Significance of Unity: A New Palestinian Uprising," *Al-Shabaka*, June 29, 2021, https://al-shabaka.org/commentaries/defying-fragmentation-and-the-significance-of-unity-a-new-palestinian-uprising/.

12. Nayrouz Qarmout, *The Sea Cloak & Other Stories* (London: Comma Press, 2019).

13. Selma Dabbagh, "Inventing Gaza," in *Gaza as Metaphor*, 11.

SAMIA HENNI

FRENCH-ISRAELI NUCLEAR COLONIALITY

Over the course of the Suez Crisis of 1956, also known as the Second Arab-Israeli War or the Tripartite Aggression, French colonial authorities concretized the promise to provide Israeli colonial authorities with nuclear weapons and expertise. During that year, France's struggle to maintain its colonial rule in Algeria, Morocco, and Tunisia was evident, and, therefore, France believed that arming Israel with weapons of mass destruction would threaten not only Gamal Abdel Nasser (1918–1970), the then-president of Egypt, but North Africa and the Middle East at large. The French-Israeli nuclear agreements culminated in the secret construction of a nuclear reactor in Dimona, located in the Naqab desert.[1] Today called

the Shimon Peres Negev Nuclear Research Center (formerly the Negev Nuclear Research Center), the center benefited from French nuclear weapons knowledge that was being developed and tested in Reggane and In Ekker, in colonized Algerian Sahara. Whereas the inhabited town of Reggane is in the Tanezrouft Plain, approximately 1,150 kilometers south of Algiers, In Ekker is located about 600 kilometers southeast of Reggane. This essay exposes French-Israeli *nuclear coloniality* through the concomitant secret construction of two nuclear military bases in Dimona and Reggane, whose archives remain classified.

France made its entry into the exclusive nuclear weapons club on February 13, 1960, with the detonation of its first atmospheric nuclear bomb in Reggane. Codenamed *Gerboise bleue* (Blue Jerboa) after a tiny jumping desert rodent, the bomb had a blast capacity of about 60–70 kilotons.[2] This was roughly four times the strength of Little Boy, the atomic bomb dropped by the United States on Hiroshima on August 6, 1945, about a month before the end of the Second World War. France proudly became the fourth country to possess weapons of mass destruction after the US, the Union of Soviet Socialist Republics, and the United Kingdom. Such pride rarely seemed to be affected by the destruction of human, animal, and plant lives and the toxification of hundreds of thousands of kilometers of natural, living, and built environments in Algeria and elsewhere. Israel, however, had never officially acknowledged or given evidence of its production and possession of nuclear weapons, but it had publicly recognized the existence of the reactor in Dimona. In 1970, with US economic and political backing, Israel achieved nuclear weapons capabilities. However, Israel is still operating under the regime of the so-called nuclear ambiguity, or "nuclear opacity."[3] Israel became the sixth country to join the exclusive club, after China.

The secret building of Israel's military nuclear infrastructure in Dimona, which was supported by their French counterparts, sidestepped the International Atomic Energy Agency (IAEA), an organization established in July 1957 to apparently promote "the world's atoms for peace."[4] France was, however, one of the original signatories of the Euratom Treaty that established the European Atomic Energy Community in March 1957—at the same time as the Treaty of Rome established the European Economic Community, now the European Union. Despite France's awareness of the protocols of these supranational and international institutions, it proceeded in secretly supporting Israel in acquiring nuclear weapons, learning to become a nuclear power (without announcing it), and exploiting a colonized desert to build its massive nuclear infrastructure.

The construction of the nuclear reactor complex at Dimona commenced in 1958, about one year after the French army completed its military reconnaissance missions and water searches in Tanezrouft, south of Reggane. France's choice of using the Algerian desert as a nuclear firing field was not arbitrary. In early 1957, about two years after the outbreak of the Algerian Revolution, or the Algerian War of Independence (1954–62), the French armed forces "reviewed on the map all the territories then available to France that would be suitable for the testing."[5] They believed that the Algerian Sahara, specifically the Tanezrouft Plain where the inhabited town of Reggane was, and still remains, was the ideal site for France's first atomic bombs. According to Charles Ailleret (1907–1968), the head of the French nuclear weapons program, this territory was "fairly distant"—from mainland France—and a "land of thirst and fear, from which all life was reputedly absent in the immense spaces between Reggane and Tessalit."[6]

Ailleret argued that the area was characterized by "the total absence of animal and vegetal lives." To confirm this choice, a French delegation visited the United States's Nevada Test Site (today Nevada National Security Site) in 1957 and 1958 and witnessed the impacts of the bomb.[7]

However, contrary to Ailleret's statement, the town of Reggane was inhabited, the surrounding region was populated and used by nomadic and seminomadic populations, and the fauna and flora were evidently not nonexistent. On July 23, 1957, while the brutal Battle of Algiers was raging, the French General Assembly and the Council of the French Republic adopted law no. 57-820, authorizing the use of 200 billion francs for the development of atomic energy between 1957 and 1961.[8] Three months later, construction on secret sites began.

The French army demarcated an area of about 100,000 square kilometers for the preparation and execution of its first atomic bombs. Named the Centre Saharien d'Expérimentations Militaires (CSEM, or Saharan Center for Military Experiments), this immense area in the Algerian Sahara encompassed four geographic and functional zones: 1) an existing Saharan town known as Reggane-Ville located near an oasis; 2) a new base-vie (life base) called Reggane-Plateau for 10,000 civil and military personnel, with underground laboratories and ateliers for the French Atomic Energy Commission's employees; 3) a new forward operating base at Hamoudia; and 4) a new ground zero zone (zone des points zéro) where the bombs were to be detonated. All these areas were to be connected with paved roads. Whereas Reggane-Plateau was located about 12 kilometers east of Reggane-Ville, the shooting field was situated approximately 15 kilometers south of the Hamoudia base and roughly 50 kilometers southwest of Reggane.[9] Most of the planned construction for the CSEM was completed in the spring of 1960. The CSEM comprised 82,000 square meters of buildings, 7,000 square meters of underground works, 100 kilometers of roads, a water production of 1,200 cubic meters per day, 4,400 kilovolts of power in three power plants, more than 200 kilometers of underground cables and pipes, and 7,000 cubic meters of reinforced concrete in the ground zero zones.[10]

This expertise was most likely useful for the secret construction of the "Dimona Project," according to the French journalist Pierre Péan (1938–2019), author of the 1982 book Les deux bombes: Comment la France a donné la bombe à Israël et à l'Irak (The Two Bombs: How France Gave the Bomb to Israel and Iraq).[11]

The activity surrounding Dimona was so secret that no one had complete knowledge about what was happening. The main difficulty in tracing the construction process could be attributed to the fact that it took place on a number of levels: the state level, including the president's office, the cabinet, the Department of Research, and the CEA (the French Commissariat à l'énergie atomique, or Atomic Energy Commission), and the industrialists' level.[12]

As with the majority of official records on the French nuclear weapons program in the Sahara, the archival documents of the construction of Dimona are still classified, and they are likely to remain so for a while. However, there are several published sources that describe the infrastructure and spaces built in the Naqab desert, including a personal account and photographs provided by Israeli whistleblower and former Dimona employee Mordechai Vanunu, which were published in the London Sunday Times on October 5, 1986, in an article titled "Dimona and Vanunu."[13]

Building the massive, secret nuclear

project in Dimona "required materials, technical expertise, and financing that were unavailable in Israel and had to be obtained abroad."[14] It is widely believed that David Ben-Gurion (1886–1973), Israel's Zionist founding father and first prime minister, and his protégé Shimon Peres (1923–2016), Israel's eighth prime minister, engineered the fundraising campaign in a discreet operation. According to Peres, they were able to collect more than $40 million, which constituted half of the cost of the construction of the infrastructure of the reactor in Dimona. Peres claimed that most of this collected private capital "came from direct personal appeals" and "friends of Israel around the world."[15] Unlike the French government that financed its own nuclear weapons projects, Israel's nuclear weapons military program depended heavily on foreign (French) expertise and private investment, which were supposed to obey the regime of secrecy.

Part of the spaces and buildings necessary for the atomic weapons production in Dimona were built under the ground. Israel claimed that this complex was a textiles factory. According to the leaked information provided by Vanunu to the *Sunday Times*, the nuclear compound in Dimona comprised 10 *machons* in all. Machon 1 is the nuclear reactor itself, a silver-domed building 60 feet in diameter. Machon 4 is where radio-active waste is immersed in tar and packed in drums to be sunk in the desert. But only a handful (150 workers in all) have ever been allowed to pass through the doors of the real secret within Dimona—Machon 2. Outwardly, it is a crudely built and window-less concrete building, two stories high, 80 feet wide by 200 feet long, an apparently little-used warehouse and office block. Two details suggest otherwise: the walls are thickened to withstand bombardment, and there is an elevator tower on the roof that seems unnecessary for such a small building.[16]

As seen from aerial photography, it is assumed that the layout of this complex is similar to the French nuclear power plant in Marcoule, in southern France, around 25 kilometers northwest of Avignon, on the banks of the Rhone River, which has been operational since 1956. Marcoule is a large nuclear facility run by the French CEA.

To dig and build the construction and infrastructure of the reactor plant in Dimona, "thousands of North African Jews (or Sephardim) who emigrated from Morocco and Algeria, [were] hired." Meanwhile, "European Jews were slowly and carefully recruited from government and private businesses throughout Israel to serve as scientists and bureaucratic managers."[17] The majority of these employees lived in the nearby city of Beersheba, as did the French experts who worked in Dimona. The racial tensions between the white French, the Israelis, the Moroccan Jews, and the Algerian Jews (who were granted French nationality in 1870) were intense. According to the US journalist Seymour Hersh (1937–), the author of the 1991 book *The Samson Option: Israel's Nuclear Arsenal and American Foreign Policy*, both the French and Israeli employers treated the Jewish laborers from Algeria and Morocco very badly. They spoke of them as if they were "like stones—inferior beings."[18] Furthermore, the Jews from Algeria and Morocco were hired only for fifty-nine days so their employers could avoid covering the costs of benefits that would usually be part of such an employment. After fifty-nine days, they were dismissed and then rehired for fifty-nine more days. According to Hersh, "The North African Jews were 'treated like slaves' by French and Israelis alike."[19]

This mimics the labor force for the construction of the nuclear sites in the colonized Algerian Sahara, which included Saharan populations. These laborers were first called the *populations laborieuses du Bas-Touat* (PLBT, or working population of Bas-Touat), and then, based on their region of origin, they were referred to as *populations laborieuses du Djebel* (working population of Djebel), *populations laborieuses des Oasis* (working population of Oasis), and *populations laborieuses du Tchad* (working population of Tchad).[20] According to Ailleret, the French civil employees and military officials named these laborers simply PLBT; directives and reports used the acronym PLBT to refer to Saharan populations. Ailleret argued: "Correspondence, such as the considerable accounts that justify the employment of thousands of workers [from the Sahara], are now drawn up using the PLBT as a unit, a term which meant Saharan indigenous people hired by the Center."[21] He recalled that one heard repeatedly expressions such as "send me five PLBT to unload the truck," but that "at the time when everyone was talking about PLBT, almost no one, except the elders of the first times, knew what this abbreviation meant."[22]

Mohamed, one of the Saharan workers interviewed in 1992 by Solange Fernex, a French pacifist, environmental activist, and politician, claimed that there was no medical follow-up or investigation on the health conditions of the Saharan workers who worked in one of the French military nuclear bases in colonized Sahara. Mohamed said: "We never had a medical visit, neither before nor after [the detonation of the atomic bombs]. We never saw a doctor except a nurse if someone was injured. There were many wounded, even dead people. There were work accidents. There were a lot of French doctors, but we never saw them."[23] In addition to this colonial and racial discrimination, due to the temporary nature of the workers' employment, the French army might not have kept records on the numbers and names of the Saharan people who worked in their centers. To this day, such nuclear coloniality, with its purposely secret or inadequate records and evidence, continues to affect the health of Saharan and other populations.

In March 2013, following a favorable response from the French Commission Consultative du Secret de la Défense Nationale (Advisory Board on National Defense Secrets), the French minister of defense opened access to 154 documents on the nuclear bombs in the Sahara. The lifting of secrecy occurred thanks to a legal case initiated in 2004 by two associations, Moruroa e tatou (Mururoa and Us) and Aven (Association des Vétérans des Essais Nucléaires, or Association of the Veterans of Nuclear Tests), in the context of a complaint filed with the Health Unit of the Paris Public Prosecutor's Office.[24] The 154 documents include various charts and tables of air radioactivity records at the CSEM in Reggane and the Centre d'expérimentations militaires des oasis (CEMO, or Oases Military Testing Centre) in In Ekker. For example, thirty-eight documents titled "radioactivity of the air" and ninety-five documents titled "radioactivity measurements" only reveal graphs and weekly or monthly reports of air radioactivity at both sites; the great majority of these documents do not contain any comments on the data. The most useful documents, when they are legible, are those that report on air radioactivity after each of the seventeen atmospheric and underground detonations. It is thus possible to verify that all In Ekker underground tests caused radioactive leaks that were noted and measured.[25]

According to a commentary by Bruno Barrillot (1949–2007)—winner of the 2010 Nuclear-Free Future Award and cofounder of the Observatoire des armements, a French independent nonprofit center of expertise and documentation founded in 1984 in Lyon—the 154 documents include many duplicates. For example, the air radioactivity records of 1960 in Reggane and Hamoudia, following the aerial tests of February 13 and April 1, are presented in two documents dating from March 13 to 20 and from April 1 to 20, 1960, and are reproduced identically in a third document covering the period from February 13 to May 10, 1960. Furthermore, other radioactivity surveys have little value in assessing risks to staff and populations because they concern periods when no tests were carried out. Thus, for 1960, thirteen documents are available relating to daily records of air radioactivity at Reganne and Hamoudia for the April–December 1960 period, while the detonation of the third bomb at Hamoudia took place on December 27, 1960, after these declassified documents were produced. Barrillot stated, "Certainly, the radiological and biological and other

monitoring services have developed more detailed reports, but they are not part of the documents declassified in March 2013. This means that only partial or even truncated information is available, which is difficult to use."[26]

France's "nuclear secrecy" should be read along the grain of Israel's "nuclear opacity." The ongoing restrictions on data about the processes and impacts of the toxification of the Sahara following the detonation of the nuclear bombs and the testing of other nuclear technology impede Saharan and French victims and former workers from being compensated. The restrictions on data also conceal the location of the burial of nuclear waste, obstruct the decontamination of radioactive sites and matter that are freely circulating in the Sahara, hinder the writing of the history of France's military nuclear weapons program in the Sahara, and delay social, medical, environmental, and spatial justice. However, if French-Israeli nuclear coloniality introduced a new order in the Middle East and North Africa, it did not succeed in exterminating Algerian-Palestinian, Pan-Arab, and Pan-African solidarities. After 1962, these solidarities were consolidated with the independence of Algeria from France.

The newly independent People's Democratic Republic of Algeria welcomed, hosted, and supported various anticolonial, anti-imperialist, anticapitalistic, antiracist, and other revolutionary movements. Among these were the Palestine Liberation Organization (PLO), the Black Panther Party (BPP), Mozambique Liberation Front (FRELIMO), People's Movement for the Liberation of Angola (MPLA), the National Liberation Front of South Vietnam, and the African National Congress (ANC). Amílcar Cabral, the pan-Africanist and anticolonial leader of the Partido Africano da Independência da Guiné e Cabo Verde (Portuguese for African Party for the Independence of Guinea and Cape Verde, PAIGC), called Algiers the "Mecca of revolutionaries." Similarly, Yasser Arafat, the Palestinian political leader and chairman of the PLO from 1969 to 2004, described Algiers as a "window through which we appear to the West." Even though Algiers can no longer be described as such, and the nuclear threat is omnipresent, further solidarities have emerged and will persist in being reinforced.

Today Israel continues to operate under the regime of opacity and secrecy. The United Kingdom's the *Guardian* newspaper reported on February 18, 2021, that "Israel is carrying out a major expansion of its Dimona nuclear facility in the Naqab desert, where it has historically made the fissile material for its nuclear arsenal."[27] The construction work, kept secret, is visible in satellite images published by an independent research group. Even though the purpose of such an extension is unknown, and Israel did not acknowledge its possession of nuclear weapons of mass destruction, it is internationally known and accepted that Israel is the sixth country to have developed such technology, with the support of France. Maintaining a policy of deliberate ambiguity is part of Israel's colonial project, which seems to be tolerated by both allies and adversaries. Neither France nor Israel have signed or ratified the Treaty on the Prohibition of Nuclear Weapons. But Israel, unlike France, has also not adhered to the Treaty on the Non-Proliferation of Nuclear Weapons. ●

5. Ailleret, *L'aventure atomique française*, 228; ["Nous fîmes sur la carte le tour de tous les territoires alors disponible pour la France qui seraient convenables au point de vue de nos essaies."] Translations provided in the chapter for this passage and all others cited here are my own.

6. Ailleret, *L'aventure atomique française*, 229; ["pays de la soife et de la peur, d'où toute vie était réputée absente dans

57–71, http://www.obsarm.org/essais-nucleaires.pdf.

10. "Rapport sur les essais nucléaires français 1960–1996, tome 1 : La genèse de l'organisation et les expérimentations au Sahara CSEM et CEMO," 46–47.

11. The title was revised in the second edition of the book published in 1991. It became: *Les Deux Bombes: Ou comment la guerre du Golfe a commencé*

Random House, 1991), 60.

18. Hersh, *Samson Option*, 60.

19. Hersh, *Samson Option*, 61.

20. Christine Chanton, *Les vétérans des essais nucléaires français au Sahara, 1960–1966,* (Paris: Harmattan, 2006), 65.

21. Ailleret, *L'aventure atomique française*, 326. ["Les correspondances, comme les

comptabilité considérables que justifiant l'emploi de milliers de travailleurs, sont désormais rédigées en utilisant comme unité le P.L.B.T., terme qui voulait dire indigene saharien embauche par le Centre."]

22. Ailleret, *L'aventure atomique française*, 326. ["à ce moment la ou tout le monde parlait de P.L.B.T, à peu pres personne, sauf les anciens des premiers temps, ne savait plus ce que signifiant ces initiales."]

23. Cited in Chanton, *Les vétérans des essais nucléaires*, 65–66. ["On a jamais passé de visite médicale, ni avant ni aprés. On n'a jamais vu un médecin sauf un infirmier si quelqu'un été blessé. Il y avait beaucoup de blessés, même des morts. Des accidents de travail. Il y avait beacoup de médecin francais mais on les voyaut jamais."]

24. Bruno Barrillot, "Note sur les documents déclassifiés le 21 mars 2013. Essais nucléaires français: à quand une véritable transparence?" (Obsarm, February 2014), 1, accessed March 20, 2022, http://obsarm. org/spip.php?article226.

25. Barrillot, "Note sur les documents déclassifiés," 2.

26. Barrillot, "Note sur les documents déclassifiés," 2. ["Il est certain que les services de contrôle radiologiques et biologiques et autres ont élaboré des rapports plus circonstanciés mais ils ne font pas partie des documents déclassifiés en mars 2013. On ne dispose donc que d'informations partielles, voire tronquées et difficilement exploitables."] Barrillot is referring, particularly, to the 129 official reports on the French tests in the Sahara quoted in the confidential defense report "La genèse de l'organisation et les expérimentations au Sahara (CSEM et CEMO)" of 1995, which had not been declassified in March 2013.

27. Julian Borger, "Israel Expands Nuclear Facility Previously Used for Weapons Material," *Guardian*, February 9, 2021, accessed May 9, 2022, https://www.theguardian. com/world/2021/feb/18/ israel-nuclear-facility-dimona- weapons.

70

OMER SHAH

FROM BILAD AL-HARAMAYN TO AL-QUDS: RUMOR, SOVEREIGNTY, AND SOLIDARITY

I have been trying to look for a video clip; I think it went viral in 2020 or 2021. But maybe it was earlier? The video is of the crowded plaza of the Haram al-Sharif complex in Jerusalem.[1] The footage was taken from a slightly higher vantage point; the bodies of worshipper-protesters cascade out toward the Dome of the Rock. Beyond the mosque, the evening is illuminated by cell phone screens. The protesters chant not a slogan but a vow: "I swear to God that I will protect Masjid al-Aqsa." A woman's voice from behind the camera narrates a form of address. She says in Arabic, "*Shufu ya ummat al-muslimin*." ("Look, oh *community of believers*"), and calls for us to "look who is defending *our* Masjid al-Aqsa. The Palestinian people." In

her address, if not indictment, the woman filming calls forth the *ummah* (an Islamic ideal of belonging), but also more collective Islamic geographies (*our* Masjid al-Aqsa). But she also narrates a more practical tension, the reality of a community committed to defending that sacred geography with their bodies and lives.

Much easier to find are the video archives of the Peace to Prosperity Workshop from June 2019. At the workshop, global investors, billionaires, and diplomats gathered themselves together in a heavily securitized hotel conference room in Bahrain to do a different set of things with words. The event signaled a familiar, if not outdated, attempt at global cooperation, collaboration, and knowledge production. Yet the language of "the workshop" suggested a new indeterminacy, if not a draftiness, to the proceedings. Watching these videos, we might stop and wonder, *Are these drafty exchanges now the great literary salons of our age?*[2]

"To Haram" signage in Mecca, photo by author

But behind the soft bluster and banal bravado of international problem-solving was a serious attempt to rewrite history, geography, and solidarity in radically new ways. During an opening session, Jared Kushner, son-in-law of and then senior adviser to Donald Trump, described the Palestinian people as trapped in "an inefficient framework of the past." Palestinian histories of engaged struggle and resistance thus need to be optimized, unburdened from the messy work of justice, freedom, and dignity. Under this modern and magical framework of peace to prosperity, the stateless and the dispossessed are reimag-

ined as entrepreneurs and innovators. Palestinians are to be concerned with *jobs, jobs, jobs*. Donald Trump aspired to be "the greatest jobs president God ever created."[3] The "Deal of the Century" thus encapsulated a set of corporate fictions and persistent religious fantasies and hierarchies.

In the words of Trump himself, the peace plan was always already "the deal that can't be made."[4] Indeed, the cunning of "the deal" is that its architects knew in advance that it would fail. Part of the real political work accomplished by Trump and Kushner's business ontology peace process was to recast Palestinians within a familiar and persistent colonial narrative trope: the Palestinians are unreasonable, irrational, and yet again wasting another chance at peace and prosperity.[5] Kushner was explicit about his complete and total disdain, saying, "They're going to screw up another opportunity, like they've screwed up every other opportunity that they've ever had in their existence."[6] And while few Palestinians attended the Peace to Prosperity Workshop—and fewer still found any legitimacy in these and subsequent proceedings—the significant, if not exuberant participation of the various Gulf monarchies and their emissaries suggested an important and public unraveling of once presumed international alliances. While one might be heartened by the growing boycott, divestment, and sanctions movement gripping universities and institutions in Europe and North America, the post-oil imaginaries of the Gulf include forms of normalization with Israel and its occupation—some more public like the Abraham Accords and others more furtive like what might be transpiring between Saudi Arabia and Israel.

In 2020, both the United Arab Emirates and Bahrain normalized relations with Israel in what many refer to as the Abraham Accords. And while normalization agreements between Israel and two Gulf monarchies are significant, the not yet normalized relations between the Kingdom of Saudi Arabia and Israel were imagined to be a crowning jewel for the Trump administration. While political scientists, economists, journalists, think tank and security hawks write a great deal about Saudi Arabia and Israel's shared geopolitical interests, namely further marginalizing Iran, what is less appreciated are new religious, geographic, and techno-political arrangements being made and re-made in our contemporary moment. Indeed, naming normalization agreements things like the "Abraham Accords" suggests highly affective and religious grammars that are still at play. While religion would seem to proliferate in this age of great transformation and stasis, other forms of non-knowledge also abound: secrets, rumors, and conspiracy theories. In this light, I am particularly interested in rumors of custodianship of Haram al-Sharif, including al-Aqsa Mosque and the Dome of the Rock, being transferred from the Jordanians to the Saudis. In and through this move, al-Haram and its special status has been turned into a bargaining chip in the normalization efforts between the Saudis and Israelis.[7] Under this new arrangement, the Saudis would be made into custodians of Islam's three holiest sites in Mecca, Medina, and now Jerusalem. This move would further bolster Saudi fantasies around statecraft and "custodianship," the latter of which combines traditional claims of Islamic care and obligation with modern technocratic forms of management and control. With this vision, Islam's great sanctuaries are reconfigured and reimagined toward more limited projects of ethnonational sovereignty and normative geopolitics.

In this essay, I want to take seriously the role of Islamic and other religious geographies in our world of secular nation-states. I am attentive here as to how these geographies become useful for various national projects, while also holding open the possibility that these religious geographies push back against more limited secular ideas of space and sovereignty. The opening vignette, this scene, address, and shaming of the Muslim ummah is exemplary in this regard.

The archive I draw from to make this argument is largely ethnographic. My reflections here emerge out of two years of fieldwork in Saudi Arabia in the holy city of Mecca.[8] I produce this ethnography in order to appreciate these other projects that constitute Saudi custodianship in the land of the haramayn (the two holy sites of Mecca and Medina) and beyond. Conducting fieldwork in Mecca, I encountered a highly compelling question around sovereignty, one that is different from the Palestinian example but not wholly unrelated. And so, as a way of approaching al-Aqsa, I want to consider a set of confusions unfolding in Saudi Arabia—the first being a question around the burial place of the Prophet Mohammad's mother, the second being questions around the "true" location of Mount Sinai or Jabal Musa, and finally, and perhaps more controversially, a question posed about the "true location" of al-Aqsa. These examples all reflect something of our unhinged world of transformation and stasis, of knowledge and nonknowledge, of incredible imagination and incredible insipidness.

We will start in Mecca and with a very particular set of knowledge workers, members of an ancient guild known as *tawafah*, figures known as *muṭawwifin*, or pilgrim guides. Tawafah is an essential Meccan institution, one that has long defined life and labor in the holy city. Tawafah long engaged the residents of Mecca in forms of global intimacy and ethical care of and for foreign pilgrims. The muṭawwif would travel the Muslim world, learning languages and customs, often marrying into the pilgrim groups he sought to serve. I argue that tawafah constitutes an urban, genealogical, and experiential set of Islamic knowledges, one that stands in contradistinction to the largely calculative and visual knowledges that proclaim "innovation" and "disruption." Under the Saudi state, tawafah has been formalized into a highly bureaucratized and quasi-governmental "institution." Despite these formalizations, many muṭawwifin cling to the Islamic ethics of care that have long defined their guild. During my fieldwork, it was announced that tawafah would formally come to an end. It is now to be open to any Saudi citizen, operating as a private company. While some muṭawwifin understood this within a longer history of experimentation with tawafah, others understood these changes as their ultimate disenfranchisement as Meccans.

Yet like all of us, these Meccan knowledge workers were often at a loss, given over to rumor and conspiracy. During this time of economic, political, and social refashioning, Meccans struggled to make sense of what was true and what was false—what was really happening, the big picture,

the master plan. Tawafah ending makes way for a secular and normatively international hospitality sector in Mecca. The muṭawwifin I spent time with attached themselves to divergent sentiments—*Long live tawafah, tawafah is dead.*

Meccans and indeed other Saudis struggled to make sense of each other, the built environment and the geography it rests upon, but also their regional, national, and religious identities. The question around normalization with Israel is not unrelated to this. While the figure of the muṭawwif might be unfamiliar, he will lead us to more familiar actors who now stalk and study the Saudi landscape—Zionist Orientalists and Christian evangelicals tourists. These actors allow Saudi Arabia to appear open, multicultural, if not secular, while evangelicals tourists marvel at both a newly redis-covered biblical landscape, the building of otherworldly city-states, and perhaps Saudi Arabia's particular admixture of techno-politics, religion, and authoritarianism.

In Mecca, I spent a great deal of my time with a muṭawwif named Abdulrahman. He works with pilgrims from "non-Arab" African countries. He's a writer, historian, and something of a media personality. Abdulrahman turned the foyer of his hajj field office into an exhibition space. The walls are lined with framed images and exhibition cases filled with objects and images both personal and impersonal—family photos with pilgrims, an old photo of the cityscape indicating his family's now destroyed home, an image with the king; all of this alongside computer prints and photocopies of new hajj infrastructures. Outside the hajj season, Abdulrahman runs weekend tours of the Hejaz region—tours to the remains of Mecca's most iconic mountains, the old city of Jeddah, and the path of the Prophet's *hijra*. He told me about trips he took to West Africa, his attempt to intensify the once vibrant relations the muṭawwif would have maintained with his or her pilgrims. But he lamented knowingly, "I was just a tourist." Between his hajj office as exhibition, his weekend tours, and his own tourism, I understood Abdulrahman to be committed to the aura of tawafah—his historical role as a guide. Yet compellingly, while he showed around foreign Muslims like myself and the occasional religious student from West Africa, most of his clientele on these weekend tours were *Meccawwi* and *Jeddawwi* professionals. This fact narrates something to me about loss—certainly of Mecca's cosmopolitanism—but then also loss at the level of embodied Meccan knowledge.

During one such tour, somewhere on the road to Medina, Abdulrahman drew our attention to an unmarked and unremarkable graveyard that is commonly understood to be the burial place of Aminah, the mother of Prophet Mohammad. He was quick to point out that this location was in fact a decoy, set up to distract the efforts of the religious authorities who might deface or destroy any markers or signs of remembrance. Pleading with us not to take any pictures, Abdulrahman took us further afield and showed us what he believed to be the true burial site of Aminah. Soon after, we took a break underneath an overpass of the Haramain High Speed Rail, which connects Medina, Rabigh, Jeddah, and Mecca. Over thermoses of cardamom coffee and croissants wrapped in plastic, my accomplices debated whether the Prophet's mother was in heaven or in hell. Our shaded discussions about the status of *ahl al-fetrah*, or "the people of the interval,"[9] were interrupted by the roaring of the speeding train overhead. Later, I asked Abdulrahman how he came to know about this decoy location, and he told me, "Through my father and grandfather."

My time with Abdulrahman helped me understand a sense of duty and obligation that many muṭawwifin felt toward this very particular Islamic geography. The Saudi state has tried to harness the muṭawwif toward their project of state building and the inherited demands of custodianship. But the muṭawwif is oftentimes out of bounds; their concerns can exceed the state and its desire for verifiable knowledge. Thus Abdulrahman's concern was also animated by anxieties of neglect, ignorance, if not abuse and hostility, toward the fullness of an Islamic geography by the Saudi state. While Abdulrahman celebrated massive infrastructural projects like the Haramain High Speed Rail, he also said he wished the train would narrate the important Islamic sites along the tracks. Tawafah's engaged and embodied cosmopolitanism was thus hastily attached to the speeding bullet of Saudi religious modernity.

Other muṭawwifin I spent time with were less concerned with tawafah's aura. Abu Tareq, a muṭawwif for Arab pilgrims, was not interested in history as such. In and through our extensive conversations and time together in the field, Abu Tareq was constantly trying to produce for me the difference between decorative projects of historical preservation, and the logistical and technical demands of tawafah's present. Together, we read newspaper articles and opinion pieces, legal and administrative documents concerning tawafah's future. Beyond a publicly accessible world of knowledge, Abu Tareq trained me in certain open secrets. He dared me to ask any Jeddawi the price to be smuggled into Mecca and they would give me the same exact figure—*400 riyals.*[10] Everywhere government propaganda narrated the crisis of sovereignty produced by Mecca and its hajj rituals: "The correct hajj begins with a permit."

Beyond vivifying the administrative landscape of the modern hajj, Abu Tareq was a stimulating commentator on the broader transformations unfolding in the kingdom. Indeed, during the off-season, Abu Tareq did not really like to discuss hajj very much at all. It seemed to me that Abu Tareq had fully internalized modern tawafah's compartmentalization into "season" and "off-season."

One afternoon, at an American steakhouse in Jeddah, Abu Tareq and I got around to discussing megaprojects like King Abdullah Economic City and the new urban masterplan of Neom. My fieldnotes from that day read as such:

Abu Tareq speaks to me curiously, almost conspiratorially, over lunch. He tells me that Neom will give way to new kinds of religious tourism in the kingdom. He tells me that Christian tourists have already begun to filter into the country and that eventually Jewish tourists will be arriving. He thinks that much of this will happen in and around the Neom project—that certain new sites will be discovered. I push back on this point a little, wondering if the kingdom really needs any more

"To Haram" signage in Mecca, photo by author

religious tourism given their plans around hajj and umrah. He tells me it won't be enough, "*Ma biykaffi ya omar*." He's not irritated by this news. But he seems to get some pleasure out of reporting it to me. Unveiling some secret plot.

While writing my dissertation, I was much more taken with images and narratives of an unmarked secularism than with the idea that Christian and Jewish religious actors might play some role in modern Saudi tourism. And while I was initially suspicious or skeptical of Abu Tareq's commentary on new, emerging forms of Christian and Jewish tourism in the kingdom, his premonition would eventually be vindicated. In the aftermath of Covid-19, American Christian evangelicals began streaming into the kingdom as members of political delegations, as independent researchers, and now as religious tourists.[11] Indeed, these categories would seem to be blurred in these new religious, political expeditions, many of which are centered around the allegedly true location of Mount Sinai in the northwest of Saudi Arabia—the future site of the Neom project.

In a book titled *Mount Sinai in Arabia: The True Location Revealed*, an evangelical historian and writer named Joel Richardson documents his hike up a mountain known as Jabal al-Lawz. Of this he writes, "Visiting Jebel al-Lawz, however—which I very much believe to be the true Mount Sinai—was the single most soul-stirring and faith-building experience of my life."[12] Richardson is not the first evangelical researcher, tourist, or pilgrim to visit Jabal al-Lawz as Mount Sinai. In 1984, amateur archeologist Ron Wyatt and his two sons walked across the Jordanian-Saudi border to visit the mountain. Unable to obtain legal visas, they crossed the border without papers. Upon attempting to sneak back across the border, they were charged with espionage on behalf of the Israeli state. Appearing on CBS *Morning News*, Wyatt explained his religious and archeological evidentiary claims, but also the nature of their clandestine border crossing. With the help of a Saudi citizen and eventually Riyadh University, Wyatt returned to the kingdom to legally visit the site. However, researchers associated with the Saudi Ministry of Antiquities found Wyatt's claims completely baseless. The Saudis did, however, believe the site to potentially have been used as a quarry for Mada'in Saleh and Petra. Jabal al-Lawz was subsequently fenced off and protected as an archeological site.

In 1992, Jim and Penny Caldwell, two American Aramco engineers working in the kingdom, traveled to Jabal Musa and St. Catherine's Monastery in the Sinai Peninsula from Saudi Arabia. Unable to assimilate what they encountered in Egypt with their interpretation and imagination of scripture, the couple turned their attention to Jabal al-Lawz as a potential site for the real Mount Sinai. In evangelical circles, the couple is cited with making several key discoveries, namely a rock formation that is understood to be the rock that Moses struck to bring forth water. In 2015, Andrew Jones, a technologist and biblical scholar, began visiting Jabal al-Lawz after obtaining a business visa to the kingdom. And in 2016, Ryan Mauro—a Fox News commentator and the director of the Clarion Intelligence Network, a group described as tracking and monitoring "extremist activity throughout the world"—began researching, documenting, and ultimately leading tour groups to Saudi Arabia.

In these quick sketches of recent evangelical expeditions and explorations of Jabal al-Lawz, a range of divergent interests and projects is discernible, from the Aramco engineer to the "terrorism expert," reflecting a range of strategies, including the covert and the unauthorized. The more recent cadre of evangelical explorers are also entrepreneurs, many of them (Jim and Penny Caldwell, Andrew Jones, Ryan Mauro, and Joel Richardson) with established 501(c)(3) "research foundations" in the United States. Moreover, more recent figures like Ryan Mauro and Joel Richardson serve as guides for tourist trips to Saudi Arabia through a tour agency called Living Passages.[13] While these trips are increasingly authorized and "legal," for participants, a sense of the clandestine and unofficial remains important. As one testimonial from the Living Passages YouTube account says:

> There's a real sense of adventure that's out here that's unlike the many times I've been to Israel or other places where history is well documented and you're reading the kiosk. It's amazing to be in a place where there's no sidewalks and there's no signs. It's a bit of a mystery, but a whole lot of intrigue as you're walking and coming to these hills. And you're questioning like were the last feet to touch this rock Elijah's?[14]

A sense of how transformative these encounters are for participants is discernible here. Again, we might return to Joel Richardson's account of his time at Jabal al-Lawz as

"the most soul-stirring" and "faith-building experience" of his life. But these contemporary accounts have deep historical resonances—trafficking between images and ideas of pilgrimage and the anthropological expedition. Indeed, scholars like Edward Said have written importantly about the relationship between travel narratives, mobility, and forms of colonial domination.[15] More recently, scholars like Rebecca Stein have written about how post-Oslo Israeli tourism in the "Arab World" produced new proximities but also new spatial and geographic understandings of Israel's place within the region.[16] But the newly deracinated, consumptive, and largely secular relationships of Israeli tourists to "the Arab" are of a different sort than those of the American evangelical tourist-archeologist.

Evangelical Zionists maintain that the settler-colonial nation-state of Israel is biblical prophecy. While this prophecy is based strongly on eschatology, where Jewish control of the Holy Land hastens the rapture, it has had a significant material impact in terms of the Israeli settler-colonial project. Christian Zionists have engaged in a range of practices that exceed tourism as such—everything from supporting questionable archeological research in Silwan to funding Israeli settlements in the West Bank and providing vibrant support for the American Israel Public Affairs Committee (AIPAC). But, as the aforementioned testimony makes clear, Israel has become a white-box museum with a history too clearly elucidated and defined by "kiosks," "signs," and "sidewalks." It leaves very little in the way of an imaginative project. But Saudi neglect or disagreement over the status of Jabal al-Lawz enables a certain productive fiction—the fantasy of a dangerous first encounter and scientific discovery.

The status and transformation of the Saudi state is also interpreted and understood in and through religious prophecy and the miraculous. As Joel Richardson writes:

> The time is ripe. Within the sovereignty of God, I fully believe that the season has come in which Jebel al-Lawz will finally be fully opened not only to archeologists but to the whole world. As this book is being written, there are plans to build a massive "city-state" called Neom throughout the entire western Tabuk region along the Red Sea where the mountain sits.

If current plans continue, the Saudi Kingdom will soon be opening to tourism for the first time in its history. Is the sovereign hand of God at work?[17]

Thus Saudi Arabia's megaproject of Neom and the remarkable easing of its visa restrictions are keenly positioned not only to restore Sinai, but also to redeem the unbelieving masses. The rhythms of Saudi Arabia's reform authoritarianism are thus not understood through political economic analyses, but rather through these religious grammars of biblical salvation. And while evangelicals do not afford the Saudi state territorial gains in the same way they do in the context of Israeli settler colonialism, they nevertheless help resolve certain crises of sovereignty in our secular age.

In 2019, close to the 18th anniversary of 9/11, a delegation of evangelicals met with the crown prince Mohammad bin Salman. This in fact was the second delegation of evangelicals to meet with the crown prince. As a press release from the delegation notes, "While it may surprise some that we would choose the week of September 11 to visit the Kingdom, we actually feel there is no more appropriate time to focus on where the Kingdom must go, can go and where we believe it is going." Clearly, the delegates understand themselves as playing an important role in guiding Saudi Arabia's reform authoritarianism. None of this is unrelated to a Christian Zionist project. In an interview about his meeting with the crown prince, the American Israeli evangelical novelist Joel Rosenberg established their objectives as such:

> Number one, we love Israel. We love the Jews. You can't shake us on that. It's because it's theological to us. It's not political. Two, Jesus commands us to love our neighbors. So, we do love Palestinians. We do love Arabs. We do love Muslims. It's not either or. But, third, we're looking as we pray for the peace of Jerusalem, who will be the next Arab leader to make peace, even if the Palestinian leadership is not ready.[18]

Evangelical forays into Saudi Arabia clearly reflect a Christian Zionist agenda, where Saudi Arabia stands in as an intermediary between the Israelis and the Palestinians, a way of further establishing Jewish control of Jerusalem and the Holy Land. Perhaps at another level, evangelicals might also be impressed by Saudi Arabia's seeming commitments to religion and authoritarian control. But for the Saudis, the American evangelicals are also strategic intermediaries, a fail-safe backdoor to Donald Trump's White House. Moreover, Saudi-evangelical relations also do important public relations work, whereby engagement with conservative Christian groups in the United States allows the Saudi state to frame itself as tolerant, open, multicultural, if not secular. Saudis are framed as "peace-loving," while Palestinians are once again vilified.

While the arrival of this new, savvy cadre of evangelicals might strike us as a decidedly new challenge for the Saudi state, I would maintain that Saudi Arabia has a much deeper history of managing religious difference. In relying on Islamic idioms of "custodianship," the Saudi state has had to make a seemingly earnest attempt at religious tolerance in places like Mecca and Medina.[19] But what remains to be seen is how Saudi Arabia will ultimately respond to evangelical scholarship, archeology, and continued visitation practices in and around Jabal al-Lawz. Will the Saudis rebuke the evangelical scholarship through forms of secular reason? Or will they allow for a robust tourism or even pilgrimage infra-structure to develop there? Indeed, Jabal al-Lawz's location in the megaproject of Neom produces new conditions and possibilities, none of which are lost on the evangelicals at the gates of the mountain.

So far, we've encountered two "subaltern" strategies and confusions around place and space—the first being the muṭawwif and the decoy of the location of the Prophet's mother's tomb and the second being evangelical concerns around the "true" location of Mount Sinai. The first betrays a set of conflicts between the figure of the Meccan and the Saudi nation-state. The second reflects a set of pleasures associated with knowledge production and first encounter, while also securing a Zionist project in Israel and upholding reform authoritarianism in Saudi Arabia. The final confusion or

mistake around geography I want to turn to concerns the "true" location of al-Aqsa Mosque.

In November 2020, a Saudi lawyer named Osama Yamani published an article titled, "Where Is Al-Aqsa Located?" in *Okaz*, a Saudi publication.[20] In the article, Yamani suggested that al-Aqsa Mosque was likely to be situated in modern-day Saudi Arabia, between Mecca and Ta'if, in an area known as Ja'raneh. In his article, Yamani advances what for many are Zionist and Orientalist tropes. He asserts that Jerusalem's original name is "Urshalim." He maintains that Jerusalem was not called "al-Quds" during the time of the Prophet Mohammad, nor is there consensus around its status as the first *qiblah,* or direction of

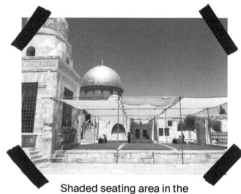

Shaded seating area in the Noble Sanctuary in Jerusalem, photo by Mahdi Sabbagh, 2018

Islamic prayer. Yamani claims that Mecca was always the first qiblah and that political actors like 'Abd al-Malik bin Marwān tried to distract from Meccan pilgrimage. Yamani also relies on early Islamic histo-riographies (al-Azraqi and al-Waqidi) and the coincidence of a mosque being referred to as al-Aqsa located on the furthest edge of the Meccan *haram* (the edge of the Islamic sanctuary), which leads Yamani to then suggest that the "true" al-Aqsa is there somewhere on the outskirts of Mecca. He closes his article with the following statement: "The lesson we can learn from the differences between these traditions and narrations is that political issues were exploited for the sake of events, issues, and positions that have nothing to do with faith and worship."[21]

Yamani's article was widely criticized both in and outside of Saudi Arabia. On Twitter some commentators disregarded it as mere "clickbait" for *Okaz* newspaper. Others saw something more pernicious in Yamani's text, a gesture toward an extreme Zionist discourse from within the Saudi-Islamic media sphere. I would posit that instead of merely being "clickbait" or a dog whistle to the Israelis, the article can also be read as a test balloon, a leak of sorts, a hazy attempt at establishing desire and then, with luck, coordinating action. Abu Tareq would frequently point out and identify such test balloons in the Saudi media as it referred to tawafah and its transformation. He would tell me, "It's about seeing what is possible, *ya Omar*." Thus we should also appreciate how this article addressed itself to and worked on a Saudi public. Moreover, during this time of tremendous social, political, economic, and ecological upheaval, there might be a very real glimmer of the possible that allows geographies to shift. Of course, the failure of Yamani's article is that it lacks any real social support or substance. And while much happens in a place like Saudi Arabia without social support or consent, the total rearrangement of an Islamic geography is too significant.

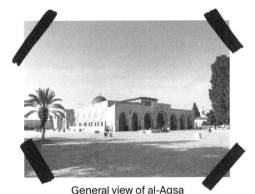

General view of al-Aqsa Mosque in Jerusalem, photo by Mahdi Sabbagh, 2019

While religious geographies set certain limits on what is possible, the secular state nevertheless tries to harness and shape those geographies in particular ways. And while I don't see Saudi Arabia embracing Yamani's proposition, the rumors and concerns raised in and through the Deal of the Century appear far more concerning. The actual text of the *Peace to Prosperity* plan establishes a set of contradictions. First, it establishes that after 1967, Israel took control over "all of Jerusalem" and the protection of all the city's holy sites, including "the Temple Mount/Haram al-Sharif" and "the Muslim holy shrines." The plan then proceeds with the following:

> Given this commendable record for more than half a century, as well as the extreme sensitivity regarding some of Jerusalem's holy sites, we believe that this practice should remain, and that all of Jerusalem's holy sites should be subject to the same governance regimes that exist today. In particular the status quo at the Temple Mount/Haram al-Sharif should continue uninterrupted.[22]

This question around the "status quo" is important, for the *Peace to Prosperity* plan makes no reference to the current custodians of the Haram al-Sharif: Hashemite rulers of Jordan. Indeed, the Jordanians have maintained custodianship over Jerusalem's Islamic and Christian holy sites since 1924, when the Hashemite Sharif of Mecca, Hussein bin Ali, was elected by the Supreme Muslim Council of Mandatory Palestine as "custodian." This custodianship has been recognized by Israel in practice and also stipulated legally through various peace agreements with the Jordanians.[23] The American peace plan thus insists on the "status quo" while eliding Jordanian custodianship. And while many expressed concerns around full Israeli sovereignty over the Haram al-Sharif and the implications this might entail, others foreshadowed that Saudi Arabia was being set up to replace the Jordanians as custodians of the Haram al-Sharif complex.[24]

Custodianship of al-Aqsa is now imagined as a bargaining chip in normalizing relations between Saudi Arabia and Israel. This move would displace and certainly anger the Jordanians and Palestinians. In displacing the Jordanians as the custodians of the holy sites in Jerusalem, the Saudis enact a certain historical repetition of their foundational coup in Mecca. But they also secure their position as the premier custodians of Islam's three holiest sites—Mecca, Medina, and Jerusalem. This would be a move that secures Saudi Arabia's status as "Islamic," while at the same time enabling projects of ethnonational sovereignty in the United States, Israel, and in Saudi Arabia itself. Again, Saudi Arabia's articulation of "Islamic custodianship" is

a complex arrangement of religious and secular knowledges, which includes both the techno-political and the *shari'i*.[25] For now, Saudi custodianship of Jerusalem is merely a rumor, but its immanence should inspire us to take its features seriously.

The techno-political and religious flattening of Mecca, Medina, and Jerusalem should also inspire important forms of social solidarity. The nature and degree of that flattening of course differ in Saudi Arabia and in Palestine. In Mecca, the deep archive of Islamic history is edited out of the built environment and increasingly out of the natural environment itself.[26] Ordinary Meccans are displaced with varying degrees of care, concern, and compensation, depending on their status as "citizens," "residents," and "refugees." Importantly, displacement in Mecca also works through intensification of Islamic ritual. As one engineer lamented to me, "They are turning Mecca into an airport." Displacement in Mecca does not necessarily match the displacements of the settler-colonial state in Jerusalem and Palestine at large. Displacement in Palestine, and Jerusalem acutely, hinges on Zionist supremacy and settler-colonial tactics of expansionism, while displacement in Mecca hinges upon grammars of speed, intensity, and logistics. The slow, entangled, and Islamic hospitality of the muṭawwif is then made over into a secular hospitality governed by the International Organization for Standardization (ISO) and packaged tours. Moreover, concepts from settler-colonial situations like "indigineity" at best make little sense and at worst play a role in devastating the cosmopolitan lifeways of places like Mecca and Medina. Indeed, it is common among ethnonationalist factions

"To Haram" signage in Mecca,
photo by author

from the crowd of protesters vowing to defend al-Aqsa to the corporate magic of the Peace to Prosperity Workshop; from the gravesite(s) of the Prophet's mother to Neom and back to the outskirts of the holy city of Mecca. These scenes narrate in different ways the power and limitations of our imaginations; they are sometimes religious and sometimes conspiratorial. In bringing these divergent scenes together it is not my intention to make them all equal. While I believe we should take seriously evangelical and Christian Zionist discourses, their attachments and commitments to the nation-state make me highly suspicious, if not antagonistic, to these visions of the future. Moreover, it should be plain that I am also antagonistic toward how the Saudi state has made Islamic ritual into a resource for the cash- and legitimacy-strapped nation-state.

But I do think there are possibilities within Islamic and religious solidarities and geographies in ways that exceed our secular imaginaries—I've tried to show this through my attention to vocabularies like the "ummah" and the "haram," but also to figures like the muṭawwif. In all of these, I see a spark beyond the nation-state. It is a spark that unites Mecca, Medina, and Jerusalem. It is a spark that gives us another way of imagining and organizing social difference. ●

within Saudi Arabia to speak of Mecca's immigrant and refugee populations as a colonial occupation—ʾiḥtilal.[27] Therefore, while there are significant differences in how a place like Mecca and a place like Jerusalem are flattened—to say nothing of the political responses to that flattening— these differences should not preclude robust and entangled forms of social solidarity and obligation. It is an obligation that for some of us might emerge from more secular categories, experiences, and analytics. But for many others, religious geographies, sensibilities, and experiences also offer a robust and serious way of imagining belonging beyond the nation-state.

This essay has tried to piece together a set of divergent scenes and settings,

ENDNOTES

1. الحرم الشريف or The Noble Sanctuary, also known amongst Jewish Israelis and evangelical Christians as the "Temple Mount."

2. In asking this question, I echo the novelist Tom McCarthy. His excellent novel *Satin Island* focuses in part on the relationship between the corporation and narrative. His most recent novel, *The Making of Incarnation*, more directly focuses on the real unreal quality of a corporate symposium. See Tom McCarthy, *Satin Island* (New York: Random House, 2015); and Tom McCarthy, *The Making of Incarnation* (New York: Alfred A. Knopf, 2021).

3. Donald Trump said this as he announced his bid for the Republication Party nomination in 2015. Dan Stewart, "Yes, Donald Trump Is Running for President," *Time Magazine*, June 16, 2015, https://time.com/3922656/donald-trump-announcement.

4. In an interview with the *Wall Street Journal* from November 11, 2016, Donald Trump described brokering peace between the Israelis and the Palestinians as "the ultimate deal." He continued to describe himself and the deal as such, "As a deal maker, I'd like to do . . . the deal that can't be made. And do it for humanity's sake." Monica Langley and Gerard Baker, "Donald Trump, in Exclusive Interview, Tells WSJ He Is Willing to Keep Parts of Obama Health Law," *Wall Street Journal*, November 11, 2016, https://www.wsj.com/articles/donald-trump-willing-to-keep-parts-of-health-law-1478895339.

5. Marc Owen Jones explores these colonial framings of the Deal of the Century in a short piece for *Middle East Eye*. These framings include an ahistorical presentism but also victim-blaming and emotional blackmail. See Marc Owen Jones, "Jared Kushner: The Colonial Mindset behind His So-Called 'Peace Plan,'" *Middle East Eye*, February 3, 2020, https://www.middleeasteye.net/opinion/trump-kushner-deal-all-about-stigmatising-palestinians.

6. Matt Stieb, "Jared Kushner: Palestine Could Botch Peace Deal Like 'Every Other Opportunity . . . in Their Existence,'" *New York Magazine*, January 29, 2019, https://nymag.com/intelligencer/2020/01/jared-kushner-expects-palestine-to-screw-up-his-peace-deal.html.

7. It should be noted that Saudi normalization with Israel is not a given. Indeed, there is significant opposition to normalization within the kingdom itself. For example, a common hashtag used on Saudi Twitter (and in the Arabic-speaking world at large) features the slogan "Normalization Is Betrayal." Yet currently without formal and public ties, more shadowy relations between Israel and Saudi Arabia are transpiring, whether that is through Israeli use of Saudi airspace, the commercial sale of Israeli spyware, or high-level Saudi public officials writing in Israeli newspapers.

8. I conducted this fieldwork in Jeddah and Mecca between 2017 and 2019.

9. "*Ahl al-fetrah*" refers to the people of time period or interval between Jesus and Mohammad.

10. Saudi citizens and residents are only legally permitted to make hajj every five years. A security checkpoint that surrounds the boundary of the sanctuary sorts and controls access to the sanctuary during peak hajj and umrah seasons. For many, especially residents of Mecca and Jeddah, this administrative feature is highly controversial, as many believe that the government cannot deny them access to hajj or the Meccan sanctuary more generally. Thus, a cottage industry around pilgrim smuggling has emerged, offering clandestine services to both citizens and foreign residents of the kingdom.

11. There is of course a deep history of colonial actors and foreign experts engaging with the Arabian Peninsula, from British colonial agents like

Richard Burton to Aramco. It is my point that more recent evangelical engagements with the Arabian Peninsula draw from and enact these histories.

12. Joel Richardson, *Mount Sinai in Arabia: The True Location Revealed* (Enumclaw, WA: Wine Press, 2018), 2.

13. Living Passages also runs tour groups to Israel, Jordan, Egypt, Ethiopia, and South Africa. They also run a "Reformation Europe" and "United States Creation" tour.

14. Living Passages, "Saudi Arabia Christian Travel Testimonial: Maury [2019]," May 31, 2022, 0:36, https://youtu.be/pVgRkugJJjc.

15. Edward Said, *Orientalism* (New York: Pantheon, 1978).

16. Rebecca Stein, *Itineraries in Conflict: Israelis, Palestinians, and the Political Lives of Tourism* (Durham, NC: Duke University Press, 2008.)

17. Richardson, *Mount Sinai in Arabia*, 9.

18. Tony Perkins, "Award Winning Author Joel Rosenberg Previews His New Book, 'Enemies and Allies,'" May 31, 2022, 5:44, https://youtu.be/ta_4fnQVL8I.

19. Mecca and Medina are of course the scene of massive and fundamental erasures. I am in no way interested in downplaying those erasures. But at the same time, I think we must take seriously how Saudi Arabia is fashioning itself as "multicultural" and "open" while continuing to edit and erase Islamic history and belonging in Mecca, Medina, and beyond.

20. Osama Yamani, "Where Is Al-Aqsa Located?" November 13, 2020, https://www.okaz.com.sa/articles/authors/2048070.

21. Yamani, "Where Is Al-Aqsa Located?"

22. United States of America, *Peace to Prosperity: A Vision to Improve the Lives of the Palestinian and Israeli People*, January 2020, https://trumpwhitehouse.archives.gov/wp-content/uploads/2020/01/Peace-to-Prosperity-0120.pdf, 16.

23. It should be noted that Israel has tried to challenge and limit that custodianship whenever possible.

24. Israeli sovereignty would further inhibit Palestinian mobility, right to worship and access to religious sites. More devastatingly, it might mean the destruction of the site itself, as right-wing ultranationalist factions in Israel would like to see the Haram cease to function as an Islamic site.

25. Some have questioned the possibility of Saudi Arabia occupying this role as "custodian" of Jerusalem's Islamic sites due to its lack of contiguous land. But the Ottomans were also custodians of Mecca and Medina all the way from Istanbul. And then more vibrantly in the present, we've seen the normative nation-state reworked in and through Israel's entire settler-colonial project—the geographic proposals within the Deal of the Century are no exception. In Saudi Arabia, the Neom project also underscores new arrangements of national sovereignty, a wholly new legal regime, and the incorporation of Jordanian and Egyptian lands and waters.

26. For an account of the built environment as an archive, see Rosie Bsheer's wonderful book *Archive Wars*. In her text, Bsheer offers a comparative study of the politics of history, archives, and the built environment in Saudi Arabia. She compares Mecca's bulldozed modernity to Riyadh's furious preservation. See Rosie Bsheer, *Archive Wars: The Politics of History in Saudi Arabia* (Stanford: Stanford University Press, 2020)

27. In 2013, none other than Jamal Khashoggi published a short booklet titled, *The Occupation of the Saudi Market*.

KAREEM RABIE

EVERYWHERE IN THE WORLD THERE IS A CHINATOWN; IN CHINA THERE IS A KHALILTOWN

E veryone in Hebron seems to have a cousin or former classmate who has been to China. People suggest "there is a *Khalil* embassy in China," there are "streets and streets" of Khalilis, and it is easier to find stuffed lamb neck, a particularly Hebronite dish, in China than in Ramallah.[1] Throughout the West Bank over the last ten or fifteen years, there has been discussion of the link between businessmen in Hebron and China. Hebron was formerly the hub of light industry in the West Bank, and Hebronites tend to be known around the region for their industriousness. Hebron is today the West Bank's most militarized and violently occupied city. News on Palestinian industry describe family businesses destroyed by "cheap Chinese imports" and

bemoan the lack of domestic production, especially of heritage items like the *kuffieh*. There are jokes: a dopey importer was stuck with a container's worth of too-big brassieres. He pivoted, altered the bras, and smuggled them across the 1967 Green Line to try to make a mint in the kippah market.

A well-established Palestinian importer in Yiwu, China, reported it was originally uncomfortable, but there are now Arabs who reside there, translators, and restaurants. Chinese diplomats are said to routinely travel from Israel to West Bank cities to give out visas. A 2008 *New York Times* piece described Yiwu, a city of 1.2 million people known for its massive market for small commodities, as "a buzzing trading spot thanks to the influx of Middle Eastern money . . .

a hub for selling made-in-China Arabic products, like fashion clothing and religious artefacts." Ahmad Kayed, then Palestinian head of trade relations in Beijing, estimated imports from China going directly or through Israel at $2 billion annually. He told the *Times* he believed that over two hundred Palestinian businessmen had settled in China over the previous decade, and thousands of others traveled there frequently.[2] The Hebron Chamber of Commerce tries to monitor the link, but there have been no formal studies to date, and what is known is still largely anecdotal.

"Learn Chinese" sign, Yiwu,
photo by Sarah Cassidy, 2015

In 2015 and again in 2017, I traveled between Ramallah and Hebron in the West Bank and Beijing, Shanghai, Yiwu, and Guangzhou in China for preliminary research on these links, to attempt to index the jokes and the stories, and to try to understand how economic and political imperatives intertwine as matters of identity, social life, and geography. This piece is the beginning of an approach that toggles from the material to the abstract by looking at social, cultural, and mercantile relationships outward and alongside the specifying

functions of the Israeli state and colonial territorial imperatives. The circulation of goods, capital, and people began to reveal geoeconomic and geopolitical phenomena that are coconstituted by forms of national and personal aspirations and identity.

The View from Palestine
On a walk home from dinner in Palestine in 2015, I started chatting about this work with my friends the anthropologist Ala Alazzeh and his daughter Nala. I told Ala I had been tracking the jokes and stories about the link between Palestine and China for years and occasionally following up with people who said they had gone or wanted to go. I said, "Once you see it, you find it everywhere."

So he started asking everyone about China. At the kebab place: "Where do you get these containers? From China?"

"No, I did, but these Israeli ones are better."

Buying a pack of cigarettes from a former student: "Kareem is about to go to China, do you know anything about Hebron and China?"

"Yes! You know, there's a village there that's all Hebronites, a second Hebron."

"Why?"

"They went so much that they bought apartments and started their own little Hebron . . . but in China."

"Really?"

"Yeah, and I'm going to go in two years *insha'allah*."

For business, his friend chimed in: "You know, in China they think Hebron is its own country, not a part of Palestine."

Around the corner at the Nahda gas station, Ala asked: "Is this stuff for sale from China?"

"Mostly it's not, it's from India, Turkey, and Portugal, but some is from China."

"I'm about to go on vacation to China, to see some factories. Do you know people there? Where in Palestine are they from?"

"Mostly they're from Hebron."

"Why Hebronites?"

"They have a 'commercial mind.' Whether they're educated or not, they're like computers, they're just knowledgeable about markets. Everywhere in the world there is a Chinatown; in China there is a Khaliltown," he said.

On that same trip to Palestine, I interviewed one of the leaders of the Hebron Chamber of Commerce and asked, "Why Hebron?" While this is not, he believes, a uniquely Hebron phenomenon, people there were well positioned to capitalize on it. First, there is low public sector employment in Hebron and strong kin networks—and relative independence from the PA—as

Palestine merchandise, Yiwu, photo by Sarah Cassidy, 2015

well as significant expertise and trade relationships owing to the city's past as a center of industry.

The 1994 Paris Protocol, the economic agreement signed in parallel with the Oslo Accords, opened the Occupied Territories to investment and importation beyond Israel. Before Paris, there were only two tracks: internal trade between the West Bank and Gaza and trade with Israel. There was little to no possibility for Palestinian-led direct import, nor direct export. *Everything* moved through Israel and Israeli channels, and at high cost. After 1994, direct imports and exports became possible through Israeli ports and with the cooperation of some Israeli dealers. There was a wide transformation in trading patterns and trends, and the "1994 era" was when people started to think about trade with China, as well as the wider Arab region. At that time Israel did not import much from China—primarily working with the US and the EU—giving the trade link to China a slight Arab cast.

Also in the mid-1990s, as Palestinians and Israelis were shaping that agreement, the globe saw a rapid increase in transport efficiencies and containerization, along with NAFTA, pre-9/11 celebratory narratives about globalization, and an intensification of uneven geographical development (a kind of planetary division of production and consumption enabled by the circulation of goods and capital).[3] In China, Deng Xiaoping moved the nation toward liberalization in 1992 alongside efforts to consolidate industrial production in special zones, such as in Guangdong Province.

Yet in Palestine, neither celebratory narratives nor the Paris Protocol did much to change the reality of Israeli border control.

Paris established a customs union between Israel and the Palestinian Authority and gave Israel the right and responsibility to gather Palestinian tax revenue, VAT (value-added tax), and import duties, which it routinely holds back as a form of collective punishment. The PA is the largest employer in the West Bank and is the scaffolding of political stability and economic growth;

Wholesale Prayer Clocks, Yiwu, photo by author, 2015

when revenues are held up, Paris's political cost is disbursed downward to PA employees and their families in the form of late, fractional, or completely lacking payment. As Palestinian capitalists and the PA emerged from Oslo with the intentions to create sovereign control and capacity for importation and circulation, they found labor and consumer markets suspended as if in aspic.

Palestinian importers believe Israel allows them access to China to deliberately undercut local production and encourage dependence on imports. Factory owners in Palestine have attempted to compete on quality against cheaper goods. The occupation creates competitive advantage because unemployment is widespread and labor

costs low. Israel, however, denies the entry of raw materials or holds them to throw off production schedules and deadlines, costing importers "millions of dollars annually" in demurrage. At the same time, Israel eases entry for goods that might feasibly be produced locally in the West Bank. Internal trade makes up the bulk of GDP, and the West Bank remains dependent on Israel.[4]

Traders tell me the process is messy, contingent, and often opaque. If they are allowed entry, goods bound for the West Bank are said to take a week or more to clear customs, significantly longer than the average of about forty-eight hours for Israelis. One importer believes these phenomena to be both political and "income-generating for Israel." The PA lacks capacity to exercise control, and importers lack institutions to smooth the process or negotiate with shippers for rate relief. Regulations are strategically fluid, and Palestinian shipments are constantly held or turned away because of errors in the paperwork, including unforced errors like failing to declare personal items—"unnecessary things, flat-screen TVs, a box of Viagra, things like that."

According to people I interviewed in the Hebron Chamber of Commerce, between 1994 and 2000, the GDP of Palestine grew from $2.8 to $5 billion, which "gives an indication of the level of potential" as well as of growth during that time. But the Israeli barriers meant importation was also necessarily small scale. Prior to 1994, importation used to be the domain of bigger businesses—shoe and textile manufacturers, electrical appliance and furniture importers. As goods became cheaper and China more accessible, it grew to encompass pretty much everything but food. As trading became increasingly possible, smaller scale, and more widespread, local products were replaced. Terminal local industries didn't survive. In their place, imported goods flooded into an unregulated market without the capacity or will to exercise local control in terms of protection or standards requirements.

At the same time, this small-scale trade and relative openness overlay new possibilities for class aspiration. Trade became an opportunity available to individuals: anyone who could cobble together a few thousand dollars could go to China and import a container back to Palestine. New and existing institutions like the Hebron Chamber of Commerce, the Palestine-China Friendship Society, and the Palestinian Shippers' Council emerged to encourage trade and protect the local market in ways the PA cannot or will not: promoting technical specifications and standards requirements and aiding people with registration and permission. According to people I interviewed in these organizations, the idea that Chinese consular officials are always going to Hebron to hand out visas "is not true; rumors are over-exaggerated." But nevertheless, this phenomenon is "not sustainable development," it is "survival" in the context of Israeli occupation, which, as traders argue, is fundamentally about increasing dependence on Israel and weakening possibilities for local production.

Headscarf shop, photo by Sarah Cassidy, 2015

Beijing

In Beijing there is a small community of Palestinians, either long-term residents or more transitory, younger workers, both primarily male. The older generation came in the '60s or '70s, largely due to Third Worldist educational ties. They settled, established themselves, and learned to appreciate—and then love—China. Some of them met and married Chinese women. The younger generation, those who have come for education in recent years or who cycle in and out of jobs in the PA embassy, by and large are uncomfortable there. Complaints abound—about the food, the weather, the scale, the language barrier, the food again.

Conversations with these two generations of men began to hint at a wider transformation of material, political, and cultural ties into identitarian links. Identitarian in the sense of being a continual process, a matter of both becoming and being, as Stuart Hall put it. It is framed "by two axes or vectors, simultaneously operative: the vector of similarity and continuity and the vector of difference and rupture."[5] These Palestinians mirror trends not just in China or between China and Palestine, but throughout the world.

Since 1978, Chinese trade policy has been geared toward opening China's labor and consumer markets. China and Palestine have seen ongoing changes, from revolutionary politics and political economy to something much less so, and have experienced their own versions of global and transnational historical shifts. It struck me that there are important and unexpected resonances between Palestinian and Chinese structural and cultural experiences of change. As "the Chinese state gave up class and class struggle as a means of legitimation, it has turned to the construction of the nation as the prime means of inducing people to identify with its policies and programs."[6] From Bandung to neoliberalism, Maoism to "capitalism with Chinese characteristics," from the PLO to the PA and the "homeland that could have been,"[7] through small-scale trade, the Palestinians in Beijing experience and practice a distillation of historical changes to South-South ties.

Mustafa al-Safarini, "Abu Hadid," is one of the eminences of the Palestinian

Worldwide friends, Yiwu, photo by author, 2015

community in Beijing. He came in 1968, served as PLO ambassador in the 1990s, and has both experienced and—as the head of the Arab Information Center and through his work in trade facilitation—tracked these changes closely. His office is in a building called the Diplomatic Cultural Exchange;

on my first trip it felt like one of the largest indoor spaces I'd ever been in. Endless hallways of well-appointed sitting rooms with national themes. For what? Meetings? I walked past the rooms and up a staircase to his office, decorated with Chinese-style ink drawings of Darwin and ancient Western philosophers. He himself wore a kuffieh and sat under a large portrait of his younger self wearing the same.

He told me the 1955 Bandung Asian-African Conference began the political relationship between China and Palestine—we got moral support, and we established good political relations, but no economic relations yet. In the 1950s and '60s China was isolated, hostile toward both American imperialism and Soviet influence. And in this isolationist moment there were good relations but no tangible benefit for Palestine. In the 1960s, Palestinians started to travel to China for military training, and China gave direct food and medical aid to Palestinian refugees in the West Bank and elsewhere in the Arab world. The year 1971 was a turning point, when Algeria helped China resume a position in the UN, strengthening Sino-Arab political alliances. China was the first non-Arab state to recognize the PLO, the first to open a Palestinian embassy, and, in 1988, one of the first to recognize the State of Palestine. But direct aid, not commerce, was still the primary tie between the two.

For al-Safarini, it wasn't until the end of the 1980s and beginning of the 1990s that China began to feel the "importance of the Arab world." "Despite the Arab world not being able to fully catch up or become as powerful as China," the need for oil and desire for its large consumer market increased closeness between the two.[8] In the Oslo period, while he was ambassador to China, economic relations began to solidify. Through changes in the Communist Party and China's relationship to the rest of the world, so too has its relationship to Palestine changed. Economics has become the primary mechanism for connection, and it continues to this day; al-Safarini says Xi Jinping is good for Palestine.

The cultural, political, and economic ties are complex and productive. Abdel Karim al-Jaadi is another old-timer in Beijing, and he exemplifies the changing relations. He has been taking lessons in Chinese calligraphy and combines those techniques and linework with the Arabic calligraphic style. He ran an Arabic coffee shop for many years, importing cheese and tahini, and is said to be the first to have brought Arabic coffee to China. His goal is to present Palestinian culture and identity to Chinese people, and his restaurant was at the center of a community mostly made up of diplomats, students, and other short-term residents. He is also a local connector and fixer. For him, business was an opportunity to make do as well as to express his Palestinian self. But also, to learn from China—to amplify collectivity in work.

He tells a story like al-Safarini's: the first links between Palestine and China in the 1960s were strong, Palestinians came to study, to translate Mao Zedong into Arabic, and so on. The ties were mutual; the famous Palestinian painter Ismail Shammout was an adviser to the Chinese Academy of Art. Yasser Arafat himself visited fourteen times. But in the current period, with such political ties becoming an impossibility, economic relations fill the gaps and increasingly become the basis for multiple scales of personal relations.

Through all of this I was struck that, despite the prevalence of the Khalil-China jokes in Palestine, no one I spoke with in Beijing got them, and they were all surprised to hear about the widespread discussions in Palestine. I wondered how diaspora ties are practiced and understood through specific forms of connection and disconnection, in an instance where economic ties are more easily established than physical proximity or shared everyday culture. These Palestinians in China began to show me how economic globalization, for them, is part of the bridge over the distance of diaspora. If distance is an essential part of how people recast diasporic formation and personal or national geographies of identity and belonging, then how are places inhabited, understood, and constructed when trade becomes a primary form of connection? I was left wondering: Where are all these communities of Palestinians in China I keep hearing about? I asked everyone in Beijing: "If you are few, and have mostly been here for a long time or don't stay, what do all the stories (and the jokes) mean?" They told me that if I wanted to find the people, I ought to go to Yiwu.

Yiwu

When I was in Yiwu, that buzzy trading city with a Middle East focus, later that year, I was struck by a simple object that helped me think about links between Palestine and China: a plastic case for a Palestinian passport I saw in the wholesale mall. Number 15 on a *USA Today* list of the world's most useless passports,[9] Palestine's is neither coveted, nor—given the convoluted structure of IDs, laissez-passers, and national passports among Palestinians in

Israel, Jerusalem, the West Bank, Gaza, and the diaspora—widely held. The covers are being made in China for a tiny market in Palestine. The display cover lived among other wholesale items, pointing toward networks of Yiwu trade. Passport covers for low-end global trade partners, such as Turkmenistan (no. 21) and Afghanistan (no. 1), and Palestinian, Iraqi, and Lebanese flags were sold alongside perhaps the ideal type of universal commodity: English Premier League merchandise. Someone had to have gone to Yiwu to special order, purchase, and import them. The Palestinians who hold that passport can barely move due to the Israeli occupation, but a cheap and nonessential accessory for their papers had made a long journey, and links them to a diaspora abroad who can likely never visit them in Palestine.

The same regional political and worldwide production trends that impacted Palestine in the 1990s and 2000s also impacted trade within China and spurred growth and local consolidation there. The market town of Yiwu grew as situations became increasingly dire in the home states of its primary trading partners, such as Syria, Lebanon, Yemen, and Iraq. Traders found themselves going to Yiwu as other options became prohibitive or otherwise closed. Moreover, in the runup to the 2008 Olympics, small shops were razed as large swaths of Beijing were renewed. That displacement furthered consolidation in cities like Yiwu that aggressively sought Middle Eastern business.[10]

In Yiwu, I met the small—but growing—community of Palestinians and other Arabs, mostly organized around the Yiwu wholesale market. There are two hundred or so Palestinians, a close but loose community who celebrate holidays with one another but who have not yet engaged in large community-building projects. They like living in China by and large. As one trader told me, they "feel loved; the Chinese love Arafat." I began to see the transformation of previous strong cultural and political ties into economic and identitarian relationships, the latter strongly articulated by interviews in Yiwu, and in parts of Yiwu itself.

The Yiwu wholesale market is simply massive.[11] It is its own ecosystem; women push carts around and sell cold dishes and rice while bored kids play in the hallways.

Yiwu street scene,
photo by Sarah Cassidy, 2015

It is the largest market in the world, yet it is also somehow small. It is not mechanized or smooth, it is a preeminent site of the "low-end globalization" that characterizes global trade.[12] The *New York Times* has called it "Tchotchke Town,"[13] and it's the place to go for any small items you may need in bulk—socks, zippers, painters' tape, iPhone cases, paintings, plates with dogs on them, clocks with the Kaaba. Nearly any manufactured small object is sold here.

This is where I met Tariq, a young Palestinian trader who has been in China since 1997. Tariq's family's path mirrored my own: they are from the same area around Yafa, were forcibly displaced in 1948 to refugee camps in Jericho and again in 1967 to camps in Amman. Unlike my family, who went through Jordan and the Persian Gulf to the United States, his family continued on to Syria, Eastern Europe, and eventually to China. Given his visa and identity card situation and the punitive character of the Israeli border regime, he has never been allowed to travel to Palestine. Yet his small, cluttered office felt like it was there—there is a giant photograph of the al-Aqsa Mosque, Palestinian flags and embroidery, and small objects made of olivewood. Tariq first came to China to study engineering, but like many who trained in professional fields he did not continue. Instead, he went into trade in Yiwu in 2000 and currently runs his own office with ten employees. He met and married his wife, a Chinese woman, and has permanent residency in China.

I told Tariq about the idea that any Palestinian who can scrape together a few thousand dollars can go to China to import a container. It turns out that practice mostly takes place in Yiwu, and to a lesser extent in Guangzhou. He told me the process: Traders travel to China and meet with him. He will translate, take them around the market to find products, and then take care of the practical things with wholesalers and factories to receive the order, put it into storage, pack it into a container, arrange shipping and documentation through licensed Chinese firms, and send it on its way to Israeli ports. Traders like him tend to operate on the basis of national—or personal—ties and their unique understanding of the specifics of Palestine/Israel. Both cultural and political knowledge are important to how trade is arranged, from these traders' expertise on Israeli ports to their willingness to extend credit to Palestinian partners.

I told him about the rumors of Arabs in China, the joke about lamb neck, and our conversation turned toward favorite foods. I told him I love *molokhia*, a polarizing, mucilaginous, green stew. An old friend was living in China and had joined me on the Yiwu leg, and Tariq said he would drop us off at a place where we could probably get it. At the end of our talk, he called for his car to be brought around. We went down the stairs and found a man handing him keys to a brand-new S-Class, a massive cabin cruiser of a car. He drove us to Yiwu's "Exotic Street," walked us into the place, exchanged two words with the staff, and had quietly arranged and paid for our meal.

Afterward, we wandered through the Exotic Street, the Chojo Road area, and found clusters of Arab, Turkish, and Chinese men smoking *shishas*, drinking tea, starting coals, and setting up for a bustling nighttime street food crowd. The *Guardian* says there are 13,000 foreigners in Yiwu; this is where

Restaurants, Yiwu, photo by Sarah Cassidy, 2015

they hang out, eat, buy goods from home, and sit in the barber shop. It feels like the beginning of a solidification of an Arab quarter, a transient and international—exotic—place of their own in China.

Palestine in the World

This is a context characterized by three triangular relationships, floating, intersecting, and overlapping in different ways at different times.[14] There is the geoeconomic and political triangle—the lines between Palestine, China, and Israel as matters of organizing state and economic relations in order to solve accumulation problems at the state level. Beneath it, there is the second triangle of local practice and jurisdiction between Palestine, China, and Israel, and Israel is able to break or manage the lines both to obstruct Palestinian life and accumulation and as a vector of its control over Palestinian territory through movements of goods to and from the rest of the world. Finally, a third triangle, within China, of intra-Chinese geographical problem-solving at the state level, where questions of rural exodus, industrial development, and urban destruction combine to orient the contexts such that places like Yiwu come to have the focus they do. The questions that animate this piece, and the provisional work undertaken here, emphasize the second and the consequences for Palestinian life in the new spaces engendered by the third.

Over more than fifteen years working on Palestine, it has often felt like an uphill battle to show that theory in and from Palestine can contribute to understanding the rest of the world. There as elsewhere, politics and capital are not unidirectional, and barriers are not endpoints. The existence, productive aspects, and political ramifications of the Palestine-China links can demonstrate just how economic relationships, including supply chains, depend on culture, on "those very factors banished from the economic,"[15] because social differentiation makes exchange possible. Imagery and new forms of identity appear alongside self-exploitation, superexploitation as nodes in the capitalist relationship alongside management, consumption, entrepreneurship, and so on. And no matter how worldwide globalization is, it is localized, it makes and remakes and occurs in social space.[16] ●

ENDNOTES

1. "Khalil" is Hebron in Arabic.

2. Wafa Amr, "Palestinian Enterprises Look to China for Business," *New York Times*, April 2, 2008, http://www.nytimes.com/2008/04/02/business/worldbusiness/02iht-trade.4.11625509.html?_r=0.

3. Neil Smith, *Uneven Development: Nature, Capital, and the Production of Space* (New York: Blackwell, 1984).

4. Ibrahim Shikaki, "The Demise of Palestinian Productive Sectors: Internal Trade as a Microcosm of the Impact of Occupation," Al-Shabaka, February 7, 2021, https://al-shabaka.org/briefs/demise-of-palestinian-productive-sectors/.

5. Stuart Hall, *Selected Writings on Race and Difference*, ed. Paul Gilroy and Ruth Wilson Gilmore (Durham, NC: Duke University Press, 2021), 260–61.

6. Prasenjit Duara, *Rescuing History from the Nation: Questioning Narratives of Modern China* (Chicago: University of Chicago Press, 1995).

7. Mohammed Turki Sudairi, "Arab Encounters with Maoist China: Transnational Journeys, Diasporic Lives and Intellectual Discourses," *Third World Quarterly* 42, no. 3: 503–24, https://doi.org/10.1080/01436597.2020.1837616.

8. Mustafa al-Safarini, in discussion with the author.

9. "The World's 25 Worst Passports," *USA Today*, May 10, 2018, http://www.usatoday.com/picture-gallery/travel/destinations/2018/05/09/the-worlds-25-worst-passports/34443535/.

10. Saïd Belguidoum and Olivier Pliez, "Yiwu: The Creation of a Global Market Town in China," *Articulo*, no. 12 (November 11, 2014), https://doi.org/10.4000/articulo.2863.

11. Statistics are dispersed and inconsistent, mainly on wholesalers' sites, and although it is not a good or consistent source, Wikipedia seems to do the best job of collating and combining them. According to that site, there are 75,000 shops spread over 4 million square meters in five "districts"— enormous buildings connected by causeways. See "Yiwu International Trade City," https://en.wikipedia.org/wiki/Yiwu_International_Trade_City. By contrast, the largest retail mall in America, the Mall of America in Minneapolis, has fewer than 600 shops spread over around a half million square meters. And it is nearly twice as big as the next largest US mall. See "List of Largest Shopping Malls in the United States," https://en.wikipedia.org/wiki/List_of_largest_shopping_malls_in_the_United_States. Back in 2011, *Business Insider* put Yiwu's market at 46 million square feet and 62,000 shops. Daniel Goodman, "Photo Tour: The World's Largest Wholesale Market in Yiwu, China," October 2011, https://www.businessinsider.com/yiwu-china-largest-wholesale-market-2011-10.

12. Gordon Mathews, *Ghetto at the Center of the World: Chungking Mansions, Hong Kong* (Chicago: University of Chicago Press, 2011), http://site.ebrary.com/id/10578477; Gordon Mathews, Linessa Dan Lin, and Yang Yang, *The World in Guangzhou: Africans and Other Foreigners in South China's Global Marketplace* (Chicago: University of Chicago Press, 2017).

13. Eric Michael Johnson, "Welcome to Tchotchke Town," *New York Times Magazine*, December 13, 2013, https://www.nytimes.com/interactive/2013/12/15/magazine/15-look-china-market.html.

14. With thanks to Cindi Katz for this language and way of parsing the fields.

15. Anna Tsing, "Supply Chains and the Human Condition," *Rethinking*

Marxism 21, no. 2 (April 2009): 148–76, https://doi.org/10.1080/08935690902743088.

16. Heidi Østbø Haugen, "The Social Production of Container Space," *Environment and Planning D: Society and Space* 37, no. 5 (October 1, 2019): 868–85, https://doi.org/10.1177/0263775818822834.

ELLEN VAN NEERVEN

WOUNDS IN PLACE: FOOTBALL AS A MANUAL FOR SURVIVAL IN ONGOING COLONIZATION

a scarred tree which overlooks the
Melbourne Cricket Ground the
survivors of genocide watch
—Lisa Bellear, *Dreaming in Urban Areas*

When the Palestinian national
team was admitted into FIFA in 1995,
that single event carried a profound
meaning for Palestinians everywhere.
It was not just another piece of football
news, but a symbol of our collective
self-assertion as a nation that is fighting
for recognition, freedom, and, most
important, against all attempts aimed at
our erasure.
—Ramzy Baroud, "How a Palestinian
Soccer Player Went from the West Bank
to Europe's Elite"

My brother and I play in Indigenous football tournaments as a way of asserting our pride in our identity and gathering with other Indigenous people across the country. On the pitch we experience joy, jubilation, grief, and anger in a microcosm. It is perhaps a way for me to process feelings that are too dangerous to express off the pitch. Football is an expression of love.

Specifically, I look at spatial sporting geographies: at Israeli football clubs on land that has been unlawfully taken from Palestinians; at the targeted bombing of Gaza stadiums and other sporting sites; at Palestinian football as resistance against the "continually evolving ongoing *Nakba*"; and the challenges to Israeli hegemony as

Palestinians assert their sovereignty.[1] From this, a significant site emerges—the site of the body, as Palestinian bodies are routinely targeted, resulting in death or injury. Many talented Palestinian players have been wounded by Israeli snipers and soldiers, rendering them permanently unable to play.

Let me preface this: as a Mununjali person, culturally, it is not typical for me to write about a place I have never been to. Knowledge of place comes from being on Country and actively learning from knowledge keepers, custodians, Traditional Owners, and Elders, while enacting a consciousness of being a guest on Country that we do not belong to. "Country" is an Aboriginal and Torres Strait Islander concept, technology, and belief system that goes beyond Western definitions of land. "Country" encompasses earth, water, air, under the earth, animals, plants, people, kin, every living thing no matter how big or small. "Country" recognizes that every-thing is connected, everything is related. "Country" is also how we, as Aboriginal and Torres Strait Islander people, identify ourselves. For this reason, I think carefully about what I have to offer in writing on Palestine's space in this volume, when I have not been on Country. I was due to be a PalFest guest in 2020 before the festival was postponed because of the Covid-19 pan-demic. The announcement of the inevitable cancellation of the festival came only a week or so before my flight. Mentally, spiritually, and emotionally, I had prepared myself for the travel and the journey from my home to another place. After the cancel-lation of the 2020 trip and my still uncertain travel to Palestine, I meet Palestine in this essay in my imaginary, with a grounding of Palestinian voices and other Indigenous voices and my own implicit positionality as an unarrived (as of yet) Visitor to Palestine. Furthermore, my contribution is centered in my own perspective as a Mununjali person of the Yugambeh Nation from the east coast of so-called Australia and in my attempt to draw parallels between the spatial conditions here and in Palestine. Finally, I analyze sporting sites on stolen land in so-called Australia that further place bodies, people, and cultures under siege. Lebanese Australian architect Adrian Lahoud says, "Architects do not heal trauma, they are complicit with its production."[2]

For reasons I have said, and others I have not yet, I am finding it difficult to write about this. "This" being what is shared between my people, Indigenous people of Australia, and Palestinians: the traumas of colonization and how it is to live in a place that is colonized and occupied by a settler state.

Let me start by way of the stadium where the Israeli national team plays. This stadi-um—the Teddy Stadium, named after Teddy Kollek, a long-term Israeli Jerusalem may-or—is in Malha, an upscale neighbourhood of Jerusalem that was a Palestinian village, al-Maliha, that was ethnically cleansed in 1948.

The village of al-Maliha stood on the summit of a steep hill, overlooking a valley. The village grid was rectangular. Many of the houses were stone. A school, a small hospital, a few shops, and a large mosque. The villagers planted grains, vegetables, fruit, and olives. More than two thousand people lived here before the Nakba.

According to a report in the daily paper *Falastin*, the earliest attack against al-Maliha happened on the sixth of March 1948. By July 1948, the land was occupied by the Israelis, the village was completely ethnically cleansed, and village life was destroyed. Those who survived fled to neighboring villages and refugee camps.

Palestinian historian Walid Khalidi writes about what remains of the village structures:

Many houses are still standing and are occupied by Jewish families, although a few houses on the southern side of the village have been demolished. The inhabited houses are generally two-storey structures built of limestone, with arched windows and doors. Some houses have balconies with roofs that are supported by columns and circular arches. The school building is abandoned and its classrooms are filled with refuse. Some of the village streets are wide and paved while others are narrow alleys that are interrupted at points by limestone steps. The village mosque, with its tall, round minaret, still stands in the center of the village. It is closed and in a state of neglect.[3]

On the site of the destroyed village, the Teddy Stadium was built in 1990 and opened a year later. Arabs call Teddy Stadium "al-Maliha Stadium." It is in an upscale neighborhood with shops and restaurants, technology start-ups, a tennis center, and a basketball arena.

The stadium fits over 30,000 spectators and its leased tenants are Beitar Jerusalem (1991–present), Hapoel Jerusalem (1991–present), and the Israel national football team (selected matches). During Beitar matches, the vocal La Familia, a far-right supporter group, occupies the eastern sections of the stadium and is notorious for its ultranationalism and racism.

In 2012, following a football match, a large group of Beitar Jerusalem fans attacked Palestinian workers and shoppers at the nearby Malha mall. The mall is accessible from the stadium by the Teddy-Malha bridge. The attackers shouted, "Death to the Arabs," in Hebrew. This chant is common in almost every football stadium in Israel, as detailed by Amir Ben-Porat in his 1998 article "The Commodification of Football in Israel." Footage captured of the 2012 event looks violent and disturbing. Yet no arrests were made and the Fédération Internationale de Football Association (FIFA) issued no sanctions. "It was a mass lynching attempt," said Mohammed Yusef, team leader of the cleaning service personnel who were attacked.[4]

Nadera Shalhoub-Kevorkian, in "The Occupation of the Senses: The Prosthetic and Aesthetic of State Terror," sees the chant and similar public pronouncements as forming "the settler colonial aesthetic landscape" and that they "converge to produce a violent aesthetic atmosphere for the colonized and legitimate crimes against them."[5]

The al-Maliha football stadium's violent history, standing on a site of ethnic cleansing, continues to echo in the violence of the present. Remembering, imagining, and honoring the village and people of al-Maliha is resisting the ongoing Nakba, though only a free Palestine will stop the continuance of colonization.

Football is often described as the national sport of Palestine. "Palestinians perceive football as a respite from the hardship of life under siege and occupation," says Ramzy Baroud.[6] The sport arrived in the early twentieth century through Arab students returning from Istanbul and Jewish migrants from Eastern Europe. Football was institutionalized through British colonization.

The Nakba almost put an end to Palestinian sports. 1948 stopped the existence of approximately sixty-five clubs in Palestine, approximately fifty-five of which were members of the Arab Palestine Sports Federation, established in 1931. Schools, playgrounds, sports organization facilities, and sports media continue to be destroyed. Palestinians carried football into the diaspora, playing in refugee camps and naming refugee teams after the cities and villages destroyed during the Nakba.

In 1998, after four failed attempts, Palestine was admitted as a member of FIFA. This was significant not only for Palestinian football, as it gave the national team entry into the international playing arena and financially supported the growth of the sport, but also as a historic step toward Palestine becoming a nonmember observer state in the United Nations in 2012.

But FIFA membership is not protection. Ongoing threats to Palestinian football continue, including the bombing of stadiums during Israeli aggression on Gaza in 2008 and 2014, the confiscation of land, the

building of settlements, the canceling of tournaments by Israel such as the FIFA Palestine Cup, and the daily harassment of Palestinians by Israeli settlers. The impounding of equipment, refusal to allow players to travel through border crossings, and the arrest and even killing of Palestinian foot-

ballers are well documented. The Palestine stadium in Gaza was bombed in 2006, leaving a giant crater in the middle of the pitch. Players, referees, and officials in the Gaza and West Bank Premier Leagues need exit permits to pass through Israeli military checkpoints, which means that they are often unable to attend international tournaments.

In 2002, the Palestinian national women's team was formed. Hundreds of women competed in championships across the West Bank and Gaza Strip. The first women's national home match was held in 2009 against Jordan and drew a crowd of ten thousand women at the Faisal al-Hus-

seini football stadium in al-Ram, a town surrounded by the Israeli separation wall on three sides.

The Faisal al-Husseini football stadium, named after the late Palestinian politician, is a few meters from the Israeli separation barrier that cuts off al-Ram from East Jerusalem.

Captain and football activist Honey Thaljieh was born in Bethlehem and grew up under occupation. Due to the ring of checkpoints that surrounds the city of Bethlehem, players do not have access to a grass pitch and have to practice on a concrete court a few miles from the city instead. Sometimes the players must travel to another country, such as Jordan, to meet other teams for practice.

Reflecting on the movement restrictions that make it sometimes impossible for the team to practice together, Honey Thaljieh said at the first match: "This is important and shows the world that we don't care about the barriers and the checkpoints. We have shown the world that we can fight, but that when we fight, we fight through peaceful play."[7]

The body is the most harrowing scale. This is felt in the shocking deaths of four children aged eleven, ten, ten, and nine from Israeli air strikes while playing on the beach in Gaza in July 2014. This is echoed through the shooting of the feet of two teenage foot-ballers aged seventeen and nineteen trying to cross a checkpoint in the West Bank on their way home from a training session.

In 2009, Mahmoud Sarsak, a four-teen-year-old, the youngest-ever player in the Palestine League, was arrested while traveling between his home in Gaza and the West Bank to link up with his new club. He was imprisoned without charge and tortured for three years. Many suspected he was held because Israel was afraid that he would become a sporting hero for his people.

The nature of football is that it provides something to look forward to—a next match, a next fixture, a tournament, a qualifier in the future—unless this is taken away by the colonizer.

In Gaza, where 7 percent of people live with a disability, some who have lost limbs to Israeli bombs play football and compete in amputee football tournaments. Football is a way to demonstrate a national identity and resistance.

In so-called Australia, we live with the effects of colonialism every day. Even though I was born in 1990 and grew up in a post-1967 referendum era, my mother and her brothers and sisters taught me a zonal language from a young age.[8] I understood that our movement was restricted historically, and this had ongoing effects on the present. There were places that we were taught not to go, more than that, to not even imagine going.

My ancestors were killed en masse by British invaders two centuries ago through methods of warfare including shotguns, rifles and carbines, and biological warfare (such as the poisoning of our flour), and those who survived were dispossessed of their land. If they were allowed to remain on Country, it was under heavy duress and always conditional. My ancestors were not allowed to practice their culture, speak their language, or look after Country as per their beliefs and values. As a result, they witnessed injury to the land through mass clearing, poisoning of waterways, and drastic species decline. This spiritually injured us. My ancestors were made to work for the white man and the white woman, forced to convert to Christianity and speak English.

Indigenous people in Australia are the most imprisoned people on Earth. We are 17.3 times more likely to be arrested than non-Indigenous people. These rates have increased, not decreased, in the last three decades. Indigenous women represent 34 percent of the total number of women imprisoned, despite being just 4 percent of the population. Indigenous children continue to be removed from their families in increasing rates through a mechanism of forced assimilation.[9]

"Dispossession has put a huge scar on this entire country," kinwoman Nicole Watson says. What does it mean to dispossess First Nations people from the land? For me, it is a nightmare that I wake up to every day.

The majority of non-Indigenous Australians live through a whitewashed version of history where they do not consider themselves beneficiaries of colonization or living on stolen land. Indeed, the nation-state of Australia sees itself as a "young" Country, formed in 1901, erasing more than sixty-five thousand years of Indigenous existence. I live less than a hundred kilometers from Country I can legally travel to, but Country my family have no rights to. I feel like a ghost.

Cultural amnesia swept through. Most of our place names are replaced with names that are after white settlers or after places in England. By necessity, my extended family members have become health leaders, laborers, footballers, dancers, educators, archaeologists, linguists, and writers as we keep our communities together in the face of the heaviest of upheavals.

In March 2022, the double standards of the Western sporting world were called out. In response to the Russian invasion of Ukraine, which resulted in swift sanctions and a demonstrated stance against Russia, it was asked: What about Palestine? What about Yemen?

Throughout the Arab Cup in 2021, support for Palestine was on display, particularly through the Algerian team and fans. Algeria went on to win the tournament and players draped both the Algerian and Palestinian flags across their bodies. Sports journalist Tagreed al-Amour said: "Those who crown their victory with the Palestine flags and the keffiyeh are doing so to send the message of one blood, a symbol of Arab unity, and a rejection of colonialism and normalisation."[10]

Club Deportivo Palestino (CD Palestino), founded in 1920 by Palestinians in the diaspora, plays in the Primera División de Chile. In 2014, CD Palestino walked onto the pitch wearing uniforms with the numeral 1 depicting the map of historic Palestine, before the creation of Israel. For this act of sovereignty and resistance, they were fined by the Chilean Football Association and were forced to change the design of the jersey.

The continued erasure of Palestine on a map and in the occupied landscape reminds me of this quote by film director Ramez Kazmouz: "Remnants of Palestinian heritage still exist, if you look for them. These small clues to Palestine's past show that even if a country is erased from the map, its culture can survive. It proves Palestinian heritage is more enduring than the cities where it once thrived. It proves Palestinian culture is stronger than the Israeli occupation."[11] While crafts, such as embroidery, tell intricate stories in the material form, by hand, stitch by stitch, this other kind of culture is about bodies and mobilities and movement. Sport is an integral part of culture that continues to survive, animate and energize.

In Australia, there are four popular codes, or types, of football: association football, Australian football, rugby league, and rugby union. While Australian football, in its professional league Australian Football League (AFL), is the most watched code in Australia, association football is the most popular club-based participation sport in the country, with more than 1.76 million participants.

I grew up in a football household. What is detailed by Ray Kerkhove and preserved in local oral storytelling is that football grounds like the ones our favorite teams play on and the ones that me and my brother played on were former campsites. Campsites are culturally significant for a number of reasons. These places were used for rest, meeting, and ceremony. The campsite was colonized into a sporting ground out of convenience; its ground was already cleared from tall trees. It was well cared for as a site of significance, ceremony, and leisure. These sites are no longer freely accessible to Aboriginal people, and Aboriginal connection to this place, what this place used to be, is erased and whitewashed. When an Aboriginal player dons their football jersey to step onto the pitch and run and dance in ways their ancestors know, now, it is conditional. It is within colonial rules and regulations. If an Aboriginal player and their relatives wanted to stay after the match and have a cook-up, police would be called by a bystander and this gathering would be put to an end. It is demonstrative of what Shalhoub-Kevorkian calls spatial and sensory colonization.[12] Underneath the space of the football ground is material evidence of First Nations presence in this place, remains of meals shared, tools made, toys played with, ochre, and middens. The evidence is played upon, but the people are not allowed to claim heritage. This is the modern-day Australia we live in, where a tiny scratch of the surface can unveil the largest of contradictions.

Colonization is not linear. It is not a historical event. As Patrick Wolfe reminds us, Australia is home to over five hundred First Nations. No First Nation in Australia was colonized in the same ways. The east coast, where my people are from, was hit hard and fast. In some places, over 95 percent of the population were killed. Then there are the ongoing, insidious ways colonization gets communities: indentured labor, removal of children, social exclusion, unemployment, poor health, incarceration, suicide, and substance abuse. It breaks your bonds and it breaks your heart and it breaks your spirit.

When I play, on my Country, I know this is my conditional allowance of time on the places where my ancestors would have played freely. And when I play on someone else's Country, I do so with the greatest reverence and honoring. When I say football is important, I'm saying it is a method by which we can exist. Football has been a way I understood the world. Even sporting colors and adornments can be a symbol, an armor, and a connection. We are called the urban-ized Aboriginals, as our Country is now their cities, places where people flock for lifestyle and culture and economic flourish,

and we are forced to live off Country. But it remains our Country.

Our sporting heroes make us feel possible, they can carry our hopes and dreams. The Matildas—Australia's female national football team—currently holds three Aboriginal players: goalkeeper Lydia Williams, young backup keeper Jada Wyman, and striker Kyah Simon. When I watch the Matildas, I get carried away in the passion of the three proudly Aboriginal athletes who are playing for the team, who adorn their backs with the Aboriginal flag— red, yellow, and black.

Like the old sport—the football game played with the possum-skin ball that John Maynard writes about in the *Aboriginal Soccer Tribe*—football and many sports and games and ceremony have been here a lot longer than the colonizers. And perhaps we do not always feel whole, but we can be reminded of our sovereignty.

We feel dissonance when colonial sport takes place on our stolen land. It weighs heavily on me. The horror is not contained to the stadium itself; it ripples. The materials the stadiums are built from are stolen materials, wrongfully taken from the land and exploited. Scar trees remain and grow with stories. We still stand outside gated stadiums to get views of what was stolen and taken wrongly. But the land remains, to reclaim our spirit. ●

ENDNOTES

1. Basma Ghalayini, ed., *Palestine +100: stories from a century after the Nakba* (Manchester: Comma Press, 2019), ix.

2. Adrian Lahoud, "Post-Traumatic Urbanism," in "Post-Traumatic Urbanism," ed. Adrian Lahoud, Charles Rice, and Anthony Burke, special issue, *Architectural Design* 80, no. 5 (September/October 2010): 14–23, https://doi.org/10.1002/ad.1128.

3. Walid Khalidi, ed., *All That Remains: The Palestinian Villages Occupied and Depopulated by Israel in 1948* (Washington: Institute for Palestine Studies, 1992).

4. Ali Abunimah, "Video Emerges of Israeli Mob Shouting 'Death to the Arabs' That Attacked Palestinians at Jerusalem Mall," *Electronic Intifada*, March 23, 2012, https://electronicintifada.net/blogs/ali-abunimah/video-emerges-israeli-mob-shouting-death-arabs-attacked-palestinians-jerusalem.

5. Nadera Shalhoub-Kevorkian, "The Occupation of the Senses: The Prosthetic and Aesthetic of State Terror," *British Journal of Criminology* 57, no. 6 (2017): 1279–1300, https://doi.org/10.1093/bjc/azw066.

6. Ramzy Baroud, "Politics and Sports Do Mix: On FIFA's Hypocrisy in Palestine and the Need to Isolate Apartheid Israel," *Palestine Chronicle*, March 9, 2022, https://www.palestinechronicle.com/politics-and-sports-do-mix-on-fifas-hypocrisy-in-palestine-and-the-need-to-isolate-apartheid-israel/.

7. Velihan Erdogdu, Risa Isard, Danny Mammo, and Brian Kim, "Women's Football for Social Change," Soccer Politics Pages, 2009, http://sites.duke.edu/wcwp.

8. On May 27, 1967, Australians voted to change the Constitution so that Aboriginal and Torres Strait Islander peoples would be counted as part of the population.

9. Office of the Aboriginal and Torres Strait Islander Social Justice Commissioner, *Indigenous Deaths in Custody 1989–1996*, (Australian Human Rights Commission), 1996, https://humanrights.gov.au/ our-work/aboriginal-and-torresstrait-islander-social-justice/ publications/ indigenousdeaths.

10. Linah Alsaafin and Ramy Allahoum, "What Is Behind Algeria and Palestine's Footballing Love Affair?" *Al Jazeera English*, December 20, 2021, https://www.aljazeera.com/news/2021/12/20/algeria-palestine-football-arab-cup-2021.

11. *Lost Cities of Palestine*, directed by Ramez Kazmouz (Doha: Al Jazeera, 2011), https://remix.aljazeera.com/aje/PalestineRemix/mobile/remix/view/#/10.

12. Shalhoub-Kevorkian, "Occupation of the Senses."

OMAR ROBERT HAMILTON

CITY AND ANTI-CITY

I n Palestine, the difference in urban experiences is striking. When we program the international authors attending the Palestine Festival of Literature, we think carefully of the progression through this difference. Ramallah and its relative breathing space usually come first, establishing a baseline from which we begin.

From Ramallah we travel south to Jerusalem, crossing the Qalandia checkpoint on foot, maneuvering through its metal cages with our bags, and then to a small hotel near Damascus Gate. Here Israeli soldiers and police are everywhere, patrolling, watching, harassing, arresting. The houses are being captured one by one, festooned with Israeli flags in triumph. Religious and oblivious tourists pour through the alleyways and along the Ottoman walls while settler organizations excavate under the city, under al-Aqsa, under the houses of Silwan.

From Jerusalem we continue south to Bethlehem, the strangled city, choked by the apartheid wall that presses up against its houses under permanent surveillance from the watchtowers: a city unable to grow. Then south again, to al-Khalil, the most brazen manifestation of apartheid in the twenty-first century, its central artery sealed off from the surrounding urban fabric, dividing the city in two, its Old City under permanent lockdown by an occupying force of five thousand soldiers deployed for the privilege of a few hundred settlers, mostly, it is said, from Brooklyn.

In Palestine's disfiguration we see competing models for the city under capitalism: neoliberal bubble of consumerist distraction; violent displacement from coveted real estate; walled ghetto; explicit apartheid.

Movement between Egypt and Palestine defined my life and patterned my thoughts for over a decade. Living in Cairo, I would travel for one month of the year to Palestine to prepare for the annual festival. Returning to Cairo, I would often write about the journey, the contrasts, and the lessons, keenly aware of the privilege of being able to move between Cairo and Jerusalem, via Amman. Two cities at the crossroads of Pharaonic, Philistine, Ptolemaic, Hellenistic, Roman, Byzantine, and Islamic histories, inlaid with Christian, Jewish, Mediterranean, Muslim, Ottoman legacies whose stories have been woven together for generations. Until the late modern era, when the establishment of Israel separated the two cities from one another.

While Jerusalem is being slowly colonized by a Euro-American ideological movement and its people ethnically cleansed, Cairo is struggling under a domestic military dictatorship that is transparently looting the country. On the surface distinct processes, they deploy similar methods: segregation, resource hoarding, (sub)urban planning, hyper-surveillance, blackmail and police brutality, touristic obliviousness, land grabs, water control, and roads—roads as progress, roads as punishment, roads as barriers—hilltop settlements, cement walls, Western weapons, new museums and desecrations of the dead, the collective punishment of neighborhoods

that refuse to yield to the march of anti-history.

Driving Palestine's roads is not only a question of geometry but of race. Three parallel systems exist on two simultaneous planes: the roads Palestinians are allowed to drive on, the roads built to colonize the West Bank with settlers, and then the moments of slippage between the two, where the designated racial underclass can drive briefly on the settlers' roads—or even pass through their checkpoints. The ability to pass through an Israeli checkpoint is principally a question of genealogy but can sometimes be achieved with the right attitude. Settlers treat soldiers like they work for them—which they do. So get a friend with yellow license plates (available for Palestinians descended from families that were able to resist being ethnically cleansed in 1948) to come pick you up, put your shades on, tuck your hijab up into a *tichel*, chew gum, do not slow down, don't even bother to look at the soldier at the checkpoint, and the right attitude can get you waved right through.

In Cairo my family home for the past ten years has been a houseboat on the river. In the summer of 2022, we got an eviction order—our home and the thirty other floating houses that hugged the Nile shore between May Bridge to Zamalek and the Embaba Bridge to the north. The Egyptian army issued simple instructions: we had two weeks to pay a massive fine and then pay for our home to be removed - to where, we had no idea; or we could pay the fine and destroy our home ourselves. We chose neither option, determined to resist, and for two weeks watched as our neighbors ripped their own homes to pieces. Through the night we listened to the sound of sledgehammering and timber breaking apart and I thought of Silwan and Jerusalem and the same choice given to so many Palestinian families by the occupying municipality of Jerusalem: tear down your own house, or we will do it and send you the bill.

A diary entry, from that time:

Saturday 9th July 2022
Egypt vs Palestine. Egypt they want to transform you—into businesspeople, clients, customers, spreadsheeters, an elite that only believes in imprisonment. The Israelis, they are torn—they want, principally, to be rid of you—but have a more complex relationship: they also want to be you, *be your houses, your food, your aesthetic, your history, your relationship to the land. Hence the effort into making the Palestinian of Ramallah self-alienated with shock capitalism, to sever them from the land with debts, to turn them into the global citizens of Rawabi: the future city of no-place, connected to nothing but fibre-optic cables and credit lines, cut like a settlement into the hilltop to survey and control the land beneath it, the land no longer giving, but threatening.*

When the state finally came for our home with some thirty conscripts and ten officers, there was little we could do. I locked the door a final time, the small weight in my hand the realization I now had my own key.

The road to Jerusalem, one saying goes, runs through Cairo. That road, like so many in Egypt, has been neglected, dug up, relaid badly, and left to rot. The cultural connec-tion between people and their place must be severed. Israel's borders; the wars in Sinai and its occupation; the Arab anti-normalization policies; Camp David and the descent of the Washington Consensus; Egypt's subsequent military subservience; the dual siege on Gaza. And yet the psychic, political bond between Egypt and Palestine remains unbroken. Egypt cannot be liberated from its military rulers without Palestine's liberation because they are trapped in the same imperial system. Egypt will be ruled by US-approved military dictators for as long as they pose no threat to Israel. The road to freedom in Cairo may actually begin in Jerusalem, in Gaza.

Palestine is a laboratory for the future. Israel's systems of population control are tested and refined on Palestinians then sold on the international market. In a world of dwindling resources and democratic retreat, the future of governance is being developed and demonstrated for both established and aspirational authoritarians to see. To move through a Palestinian city is to move through an interlocking matrix of control from the tiniest of behavioral data points (a camera that can identify you by your gait) to the grandest of millenarian fantasies.

In East Jerusalem, the streets are monitored by at least 1,100 cameras that watch the Palestinian population at all times, cross-checking passersby against a database of facial recognition, biometrics, social media, digital communications, and government records to create a "predictive policing" system.[1] The biometric start-up behind this is called "Anyvision"—now trading as "Oosto"—a company that "uses deep learning AI to eliminate many of traditional systems' shortcomings, by accurately capturing faces in real-world environments, even with low bandwidth CCTV cameras."[2]

Across the West Bank, a facial recognition program called "Blue Wolf" has been developed since at least 2020, and Israeli soldiers have been tasked with photographing thousands of Palestinians and entering their facial metrics into the program without their knowledge or consent.

Unit 8200 is a signals and intelligence unit in the Israeli army. The largest single unit, it is tasked with the surveillance of the Palestinian population. A typical Unit 8200 operation would be to hack into the phone of a Palestinian and blackmail them with its contents—often sexual—and turn them into an intelligence asset.

The Israeli high-tech export economy is dominated by graduates of this military unit. A 2018 study found that Israel was home to seven hundred surveillance technology companies, and 80 percent of the founders were Unit 8200 graduates.[3] They span cybersecurity (Check Point, Palo Alto Networks, Lightcyber, Mitiga, Sygnia, Team8), data protection (Mine, Solvo), digital manipulation and anonymization (D-ID), crypto utilities (Fireblocks), roommate matching via Facebook post analysis (Homie), AI writing (AI21), AI property leasing (Knock), AI human resources (Pecan), AI financial reports (Trullion), AI medical billing (Nym

View of the Har Homa settlement, photo by Marcel Masferrer Pascual, 2007, CC BY 2.0

Health), and facial recognition for retail (Preciate).

As far back as 2014, a group of whistle-blowers came forward with details about Unit 8200's practices:

> All Palestinians are exposed to non-stop monitoring without any legal protection. Junior soldiers can decide when someone is a target for the collection of information. There is no procedure in place to determine whether the violation of the individual's rights is necessarily justifiable. The notion of rights for Palestinians does not exist at all. Not even as an idea to be disregarded.[4]

A physical and digital matrix of constant surveillance and algorithmic assessment is a future clearly being designed for all of us, and it is being refined in Palestine. This isn't new: colonial cities have always been sites of experimentation by colonial powers. From the urban design and management of class and racial hierarchies to the deployment of infrastructure as extraction, division, and violence, the colonial city attacks its host. The colonial city swells and seeks to flatten difference into a single, monochrome, "globalized," endpoint. The design of gated communities in Egypt is indiscernible from the plans of Israeli settlements, which are indiscernible from American suburbs, which evolved from white settlers' "bordertowns"—defensively structured rings of buildings facing outward, with controlled access points, navigable only by car, on higher ground wherever possible, and always in firm control over the area's water. The mall built illegally between Jerusalem's threatened Mamilla Cemetery and the Old City is indistinguishable from

"retail experiences" now available around the world. Built by Palestinian and Qatari capitalists, Rawabi is the first Palestinian "planned city" and the only major urban development to be granted permission by Israel since 1967—and it looks like an Israeli settlement. It even has the mall. Variety, polyphony, democracy, chaos—all being rolled, slowly, into monopoly. And although this aesthetic, and the politics that drive it, is everywhere, there is nothing normal or natural about it.

View of Rawabi,
photo by Baraa Zm, 2017, CC BY 4.0

The collectively written *Red Nation Rising* makes sense of this monopoly on cities and on life:

> There is nothing natural about settler relations, thus, there is nothing natural about the settler. What the settler calls democracy, we call unfreedom. What the settler calls property, we call violence. What the settler takes for granted, we seek to abolish. Abolishing private property liberates land from the borders that imprison it. Bordertown justice envisions a world without borders. We abolish borders by burning bordertowns to the ground. Without

borders, capitalism dies. When there are no longer borders, settler colonialism too ceases to exist. When there are no longer borders, we will be free to live in peace and harmony with all our relations.[5]

In Cairo, in Palestine, in Arizona, in North Dakota, a planning style defined by the control of land and resources, by fear of the other, fear of the outside, and fear of nature. An architectural mode that appears when there is something *wrong*. This is the future of the city as *anti-city*: gated, uniform, monocultural, antidemocratic, wasteful, transplantable, boundaried, fearful, securitized, surveilled, and with no question of who is *us* and who must be kept outside the gates. The city and the anti-city. The battle raging all around us, every moment.

3 May 2022
Reading Ahed al-Tamimi's upcoming memoir. Alaa [Abd el-Fattah] is on day 31 of hunger strike and I am finding Ahed's book emotional. Is there something of Palestinian sumud *that we are missing in Egypt, something that comes from us being so divided from the land? The way she describes life in Nabi Saleh, I see it also in the quality of relationship many Palestinian friends have to their own towns, their trees, the land—so many that farm, that hike, that know the trees and the plants and the habits of the animals. It is part of existing completely differently to the colonizer. . . . Egypt has it's own* sumud—*villagers who have fought off army bulldozers, neighbourhoods that break their own access points into the highways that cut through their towns, the islands in the Nile that keep fighting back,*

the sheer act of surviving at all—but I am consumed by the city, bounded by it totally. But they are razing that too, in punishment and for profit, the cement pouring faster and faster.

Driving west out of Jerusalem there is the mountain road that curves with the descent, the ethnically cleansed houses of Lifta still nestled in the valley leading down to a natural spring. And then above appears Israel, a cement highway bursting through the line, across the sky, a mechanical line cutting against the slope of nature, the hand of man stretching in concrete over the valley. The road between Cairo and Jerusalem will not be straight. It will be long and hard. It must pass through Gaza. And it must be taken the whole way. ●

ENDNOTES

1. Sophia Goodfriend, "The Expansion of Digital Surveillance in Jerusalem and Impact on Palestinians Rights," 7amleh, the Arab Center for Social Media Advancement, 2021, https://7amleh.org/storage/Digital%20Surveillance%20Jerusalem_7.11.pdf.

2. "6 Ways to Use Video Surveillance to Mitigate Risk," Oosto, February 10, 2022, https://oosto.com/video-surveillance-to-mitigate-risk/.

3. Hagar Shezaf and Jonathan Jacobson, "Revealed: Israel's Cyber-spy Industry Helps World Dictators Hunt Dissidents and Gays," *Haaretz*, October 19, 2018, https://www.haaretz.com/israel-news/2018-10-20/ty-article-magazine/.premium/israels-cyber-spy-industry-aids-dictators-hunt-dissidents-and-gays/0000017f-e9a9-dc91-a17f-fdadde240000.

4. "Any Palestinian Is Exposed to Monitoring by the Israeli Big Brother," *Guardian*, September 12, 2014, https://www.theguardian.com/world/2014/sep/12/israeli-intelligence-unit-testimonies.

5. Nick Estes, Melanie K. Yazzie, Jennifer Denetdale, and David Correia, *Red Nation Rising: From Bordertown Violence to Native Liberation* (Oakland: PM Press, 2021), 131.

MABEL O. WILSON

CONCERNING THE VIOLENCE OF ARCHITECTURE

This world divided into compartments, this world cut in two is inhabited by two different species. The originality of the colonial context is that economic reality, inequality, and the immense difference of ways of life never come to mask the human realities. When you examine at close quarters the colonial context, it is evident that what parcels out the world is to begin with the fact of belonging to or not belonging to a given race, a given species.[1]
—Frantz Fanon, *The Wretched of the Earth*

ALLENBY BRIDGE, Jordan/Palestine
11:45. I waited. I watch a gauzy blanket of clouds slowly drift across the faint blue sky. The warmth of the sun on my face was a refreshing change from the cold, dark-

gray Michigan days that had at that time structured my rhythms of waking, working, and sleeping. I sat on a bench near an exit as travelers trickled through after completing the passport and document screening at the Israeli-controlled Allenby Bridge crossing between the borders of Jordan and Palestine.

"Allenby Crossing." I wondered why the British placename persisted. It was a curious leftover of Europe's colonial occupation of the region, even though in the nineteenth century the Ottomans had built the original bridge to connect the east and west banks of the Jordan River. The Jordanians have renamed the same border crossing the King Hussein Bridge and Palestinians refer to it as the al-Karameh Bridge. The Israelis persist, however, in commemorating the site's European colonial history. This is no surprise. Placenames not only remember great men but also reinscribe power through the symbolic patriarchal and racial dimensions of nationalist mythos. Emblematic of that point, mythologized by his nickname of "The Bloody Bull" and elevated by his peer status of viscount, Field Marshal Edmund H. H. Allenby's resume narrates the scenes of late-nineteenth- and early-twentieth-century British imperial conquest: South Africa, Palestine, and Egypt. In this period, it was the British colonizers who mandated where Palestine began and ended. They drew its colonial borders to demarcate the differences of here from there, them (colonized) from us (colonizer).

I waited. The stress of a second day, a Saturday, of border crossings remained ever present. We traveled by bus from Amman to a Jordanian departure checkpoint, followed by another bus trip to the Israeli checkpoint housed in a nondescript one-story building, before entering Palestine. Rather than military border guards manning the booths, a civil workforce screened travelers, a restructuring effort to whitewash the overt hostilities toward Palestinian and other Arab travelers. The checkpoint workers represented the interests of several Israeli governmental agencies: the Israel Airports Authority, customs division of the Israel Tax Authority, the Population and Immigration Authority, and border control. The guards in charge of surveillance—mostly via camera and behind hidden observation screens—operated under the aegis of the Israel Defense Forces authorities, including the

Israel Police. It was unclear which worker belonged to what agency, but collectively they policed the imposition of a succession of enclosures—the Green Line (1947), Oslo Accords (1993), and the separation barrier (2000)—that Israel has inflicted in and around Palestinian communities inside the West Bank to enable its unlawful dispossession of land and the continued displacement of Palestinian residents.

Inside the departure hall our group dispersed as we queued for luggage and passport screening. As an African American woman, I was uncertain how my Blackness would register within this particular surveillance regime. In the United States, it typically marks my body as always already a threat and less than human. Aware of my every move being scrutinized, I listened to the border agent's questions, especially inquiries about the itinerary and intent of my travel plans: "Where are you going?" "Why are you here?" and "Who will you be visiting?"—questions that we had been advised by our hosts to answer calmly and carefully. I passed through without further interrogation. Perhaps because I fit the profile of a Black American female, maybe Christian, traveling to Jerusalem for Easter-related tourism, I posed no threat. Once I received my stamped piece of paper I went outside to wait for the others. Three hours later, just before the operation closed for the day at one o'clock in the afternoon, everyone finally made it through passport control.

We had purposefully divided the group so that we were less conspicuous.

Our hosts had cautioned that anyone with any semblance—name, passport, or appearance—of Arabness, those who had traveled in certain parts of the region, or whose work delved into issues of colonialism or Israeli sovereignty would most likely be detained for further questioning. And indeed, this racial profiling by Israeli border agents was precisely what happened. Several of our party were removed from the processing line. One person later shared that they had a quixotic conversation with their interrogator. Because their research had been profiled in the database, the agent was keen on discussing *The Battle of Algiers*, Gillo Pontecorvo's iconic cinematic meditation on insurgent rebellion, which had been a training film used by the Israeli army. Otherwise, all shared that between rounds of rapid-fire questioning that attempted to catch any discrepancy in their travel plans, they sat and waited to be released.

These delays were no doubt intentional. That is the point of border control points—to immobilize, waste time, waste lives. What I experienced was what scholar Helga Tawil-Souri—who I would hear later that day at our first PalFest event—calls "checkpoint time," or what she writes as a "disjunctive temporality [that] produces deep ontological insecurity: there is no continuity, stability, or routine. There is no ability to plan ahead, no ordered sequence, no continuous narrative."[2] It is useful to discern how this ontological instability emerges from the racial project that underwrites the illegal occupation of Palestine. Its temporal command depends upon how modernity becomes legible in relation to the ahistoricity and backwardness of the primitive, the savage, the Arab, the Negro, the Indian, and all their descendants—whose time is expendable, whose land and resources are exploitable, and whose lives are disposable.

The enclosures that the Israeli government has imposed around Palestinian communities continues the spatial-temporal order of division and dependency between colonizer and colonized that psychiatrist Frantz Fanon astutely sketched in his first chapter "Concerning Violence" in *The Wretched of the Earth*. Fanon writes, *"The colonial world is a world cut in two. The dividing line, the frontiers are shown by barracks and police stations. In the colonies it is the policeman and the soldier who are the official, instituted go-betweens, the spokesmen of the settler and his rule of oppression."*[3] Strategically placed, the architecture of these "dividing lines" can be solid, porous, spatial, permanent, temporary, or mobile. The colonial logics from the era of Allenby persist in a host of techniques, infrastructures, and architectures of checkpoints—an estimated 165 in the occupied territories of the West Bank and Gaza.[4]

When bodies cross borders, they are subjected to all forms of scrutiny. Processes of subjection—nationality but also gender, sexuality, and race—are performed, allowing agents of the state to determine the status of belonging, rights, and humanity. At the various border crossings that I experienced while traveling around the West Bank, scenes of subjection played out the necropolitical imperative of modern governmentality, which is "to make live" or "let die."[5] Racialization, in the form of racism and racist policies, systemically chips away at one's ability to thrive, produce, and reproduce individually and collectively. It may be difficult to grasp because race isn't one thing but many things—policies, ideas, epistemologies, identities, practices, and material conditions like infrastructures—that form what scholar Alex Weheliye labels "racializing assemblages." For Weheliye, racializing assemblages are neither biological (Homo sapiens) nor cultural (civilized or primitive), but rather "a set of sociopolitical processes that discipline humanity into full humans, not-quite-humans and nonhumans."[6] By dividing territories, borders function as wastelands, zones of suspended time, and disrupted space.

In these border zones—checkpoints and the areas nearby—I witnessed how the Israeli government mobilized the surveillance and curtailment of movement throughout the occupied territories as a racializing project of dispossession, displacement, dehumanization, and death. As Saidiya Hartman asks within the context of the United States's ongoing romance with white supremacy, can the enclosure of Blackness be breached or abolished by the destruction of the modern world that requires its negation of life in order for whiteness to have meaning and value?[7] The racialized enclosure, as such, is not only spatial and material, but its articulations also construct forms of psychological and bodily enclosures. Fanon writes, *"The Zone where the native lives is not complimentary to the zone inhabited by the settlers. The two zones are opposed, but not in the service of a higher unity. Obedient to the rules of Aristotelian logic they both follow*

the principle of reciprocal exclusivity. No conciliation is possible, for of the two terms, one is superfluous."[8]

SHU'FAT CHECKPOINT, Jerusalem

14:45. Our oversized tour bus lumbered through a roundabout near the checkpoint leading into the Shu'fat Refugee Camp in northeast Jerusalem. With its distinct modernist roofline and series of concrete booths to expedite vehicular and pedestrian screening, the checkpoint manned by the Israeli military opened in 2011. The Shu'fat Camp, established in 1967 for 1,500 refugees, is now home to thousands of families. Starting in 2004, the Israeli government

fig.1
Separation barrier with housing in the Shu'fat Refugee Camp in Jerusalem, photo by author, 2019

enclosed the camp with a twenty-five-foot-tall "separation barrier" even though it sits within Jerusalem's municipal borders. When examined up close, the wall appeared to be constructed like a vertical "Jersey barrier," a modular concrete wall typically used in the US to divide highways (fig. 1). This technique of faceted concrete modules can effectively navigate uneven terrain and snake around obstacles. The Israeli government erected the wall, with its cylindrical guard towers and trap doors that allow for military incursions, to enclose residents of the camp and elsewhere inside a shrinking footprint of Palestinian land. This type of border wall is what theorist Eyal Weizman identifies as "elastic," a flexible architecture of walls within an arsenal of barriers, blockades, checkpoints, and "killing zones" that can shrink and expand a territory under siege.[9] By rapidly deploying separation barriers, followed by the construction of buildings and infrastructure for settlers, the Israeli government has effectively split the colonizer/settler's domain from that of the colonized/native.

The construction of new housing populated both sides of Shu'fat's border zone, albeit erected with different degrees of durability and livability. I could identify the settler side of the wall by its orderly red tiled roofs of multiple-family, two- and three-story housing complexes on the hilltops surrounded by buffers of olive trees and terraced farmland—former Palestinian steads—in nearby Pisgat Ze'ev or Ramat Shlomo settlements. Fanon writes, *"The settlers' town is a strongly built town, all made of stone and steel. It is a brightly lit town; the streets are covered with asphalt, and the garbage cans swallow all the leavings, unseen, unknown and hardly thought about."*[10] In her study of planning in Beirut

during and after the Lebanese civil war, urban theorist Hiba Bou Akar observes the emergence of "conflict urbanism" whereby a city's future is imagined "as a time of further conflict."[11] By erecting separation barriers on the peripheries of Jerusalem, the Israeli-controlled municipal government created sites of future development, infrastructures, and profit, but also, as Bou Akar astutely identifies as a feature of conflict urbanism, sites of future war. This was evident on our way to Shu'fat checkpoint. As our bus navigated the main artery, Shu'fat Street, it drove parallel to the tracks of the Red Line that is a segment of the billion-dollar Jerusalem Light Rail project. With its shiny silver railcars linking the Israeli settlements in East Jerusalem, this is infrastructure in service of the illegal occupation's territorialization. Fanon writes, *"The settler's feet are never visible, except perhaps in the sea; but there you're never close enough to see them. His feet are protected by strong shoes although the streets of his town are clean and even, with no holes or stones."*[12] Infrastructures of light, air, water, and parkland enable residents of the settler town to thrive. Fanon writes, *"The settler's town is a well-fed town, an easygoing town; its belly is always full of good things. The settlers' town is a town of white people, of foreigners."*[13]

The antithesis of the mobility emblematic of the settler's domain, the separation barrier that encloses the Shu'fat Camp immobilizes and restricts the freedoms of the residents, who were dispossessed and displaced from their homes in Nitaf, Deir Yasin, Lifta, El-Bureij, and parts of Jerusalem in the 1948 Nakba. The checkpoint's surveillance apparatuses criminalize the community's comings and goings. Deprived of viable Palestinian governance, and of their right of return, the residents of the camp still await—some fifty-five years later—the arrival of essential infrastructures of transportation, water, health, and sanitation. The absence of playgrounds and parks constrict the play of children and the leisure of adults alike. Fanon writes, *"The town belonging to the colonized people, or at least the native town, the Negro village, the medina, the reservation, is a place of ill fame, peopled by men of evil repute."*[14]

Shu'fat's apartment blocks loom over the separation barrier. They rise ten to fifteen stories or more—balcony on top of balcony with satellite dishes embellishing their concrete facades. Because these apartment buildings were built cheek-by-jowl, their density chokes off the flow of fresh air and accessibility to sunlight. Their close proximity also poses a severe fire hazard. Fanon writes, *"It is a world without spaciousness; men live there on top of each other, and their huts are built one on top of the other. The native town is a hungry town, starved of bread, of meat, of shoes, of coal, of light."*[15] Our guide Ray Dolphin shared that the quality of construction of many of these housing blocks are likely substandard and lack building code compliance. To make matters even more precarious, these multistory buildings are built without the proper seismic reinforcements; these apartments could potentially collapse if a sizable earthquake occurred. What I witnessed on the other side of the separation barrier was a deadly catastrophe waiting to happen—an architecture in service of wasting lives. Fanon writes, *"The native town is a crouching village, a town on its*

knees, a town wallowing in the mire. It is a town of niggers and dirty Arabs."*[16] What the white settler-colonial apparatus institutes in Palestine is a racializing project, one enacted through violent territorial enclosure, deprivation, and death. Fanon writes, *"They are born there, it matters little where or how; they die there, it matters not where, nor how."*[17]

CHECKPOINT 56, Hebron
13:42. Piled high, robust heads of cauliflower threatened to tumble out of a huge plastic shipping bin. Nearby vegetable and fruit sellers used megaphones to broadcast their wares: lemons, oranges, tomatoes, and the aforementioned cauliflower—all arrayed in artful piles to entice buyers. We had paused here on our tour of Hebron's Old City amid the weekday bustle of the market, where streets converged into al-Shuhada Street, the main artery. While it may have been teeming with sounds of vendors, shoppers, pedestrians, and vehicular traffic, this urbanity, as our guide Walid Abu al-Halawah informed us, could be disrupted and dispersed at any moment by jeeps filled with Israeli soldiers. I turned around to look down al-Shuhada Street and took note of several large, graffitied, concrete security blocks that impeded vehicular access. A few meters beyond the barricade the Israeli government had constructed Checkpoint 56 after an American Israeli massacred thirty worshippers at the Ibrahimi Mosque in 1994 (fig. 2). The subsequent protests led to the punishment of Palestinians, not the settlers, by creating a geography of racialized enclosures and instituting a regime of surveillance throughout the city of Hebron. This checkpoint currently restricts

Palestinian passage from H1 (native town) into H2 (settler town). On the other side of the checkpoint resides the military zone established by Israel in 2015. The zone cordons off the Palestinian neighborhood of Tel al-Rumeidah where the illegal Beit Hadassah and Beit Romano settlements have taken possession of houses and businesses.

fig.2
Checkpoint 56 that blocks al-Shuhada Street in the old market of Hebron, photo by author, 2019

As we walked in the direction of the checkpoint the din of the market transitioned into the clanging sound of the revolving metal turnstiles installed below a two-and-a-half-story security fence. All residential and commercial doors along al-Shuhada Street had been padlocked and welded shut. As I walked up the street, I came across a multitiered cart, whose plastic compartments may have once held candy for sale

to children or magazines and newspapers purchased by local residents. Abandoned by its owner and covered in dust, the cart's compartments were now filled with discarded food wrappers, plastic bottles, and piles of torn cardboard. I discovered on the ground below the cart the gold casings of spent rubber bullets strewn among candy wrappers. Three depleted black and orange gas canisters, labeled in Hebrew, spilled out of one of the boxes (fig. 3). Purposefully blockading a major commercial avenue that was once a vital social space for Palestinian residents of Hebron, Checkpoint 56 has been a flashpoint of violent confrontations between protesters and the lethal forces of occupation—like in 2015 when two young men from Tel al-Rumeidah were executed by the military.[18]

In the days, months, and years between these at times deadly flare-ups, everyday life nonetheless passes into and out of Checkpoint 56. Palestinian children navigate daily screenings on their way to and from school. This may explain the plethora of candy wrappers among the trash. Perhaps for the teenage girl in black tights approaching the gates, her plaid backpack filled with books and other things a girl of her age might collect, the momentary sweetness of the candy becomes a welcome distraction from the indignities endured through the screening process. *"It is obvious here that the agents of the government speak the language of pure force."*[19]

We each passed through the checkpoint's revolving turnstiles. Once inside, five cameras stationed above the divided screening lanes watched mine and everyone else's movements. A guard booth perched above the checkpoint comprised the last layer of surveillance. With the added high-tech surveillance equipment, a screening room, an observation room, and the four revolving turnstiles, the checkpoint was upgraded in 2019 to the status of a terminal.[20] As I exited the screening process, I noticed a menorah—national symbol of the Israeli state—that had been attached to one of the swinging metal barriers. A majority of the Palestinians in this neighborhood have been incrementally forced from their homes by the Israeli military and settlers since the mid-1990s. Around eight hundred Palestinian residents remained.

fig.3
Tear gas canisters found on al-Shuhada
Street near Checkpoint 56,
photo by author, 2019

Along this stretch of al-Shuhada Street the military had shuttered most of the shop fronts and residential entrances. This forced displacement mirrored what I saw earlier in the day as we passed through Hebron's old *souq* on the other side of these buildings. *"This world divided into compartments, this world cut in two is inhabited by two different species."*[21] There too the military had sealed off passages and stairways to al-Shuhada Street through the deployment of a range of architectural tactics. Some arteries were blocked by metal gates with barbed wire. Elsewhere, patchworks of corrugated panels and two-ton concrete security blocks had been erected to close off the illegal settlements from Palestinians in the historic neighborhood (fig. 4). In some blocked passages, settlers dumped mounds of garbage. A Palestinian resident in the area shared how he and his family were routinely pelted with eggs and bottles by settlers in an effort to drive them from their homes. Despite being exiled, a few vendors had hung their wares—robes, hijabs, and bedding—under the metal awnings of closed storefronts, giving a hint of the area's former vitality. Areas of the market where merchants and craftspeople had been able to reestablish commerce relied on welded wire fencing, sometimes covered with tarps, that shielded them and pedestrians from caustic liquids and trash that rained down from adjacent settler buildings. Nonetheless, the tactics of enclosure effectively sealed the settlers off from the natives, turning parts of the Old City into a wasteland, zones that have obliterated life—both human and natural.

The eerie silence of a once bustling al-Shuhada Street was interrupted by a jeep filled with soldiers, followed by the shrieking accusations of a local settler. The Israeli settler we encountered was an angry one, not shy in concocting bogus claims of harassment. She wagged her finger as

fig.4
Sealed-off passage erected by the Israeli
military between the old city of Hebron and
illegal settlement, photo by author, 2019

she marshaled her privileges to direct the military and police to expel any person she deemed a threat. *"It is the policeman and the soldier who are the official, instituted go-betweens, the spokesmen of the settler and his rule of oppression."*[22] Some in our group exercised their rights to dispute her falsehoods, while others, *"belonging to the colonized people, or at least the native town, the Negro village, the medina, the reservation,"* instinctively retreated from this intense scene of regulation.[23] Some of us knew all too well that the military enforces the state of emergency while the police impose the everyday domination of nonwhites. *"The intermediary does not lighten the oppression, nor seek to hide the domination; he shows them up and puts them into practice with the clear conscience of an upholder of the peace; yet he is the*

bringer of violence into the home and into the mind of the native."[24] I joined others anxiously standing on the curb, keenly aware that the racial signifiers of our skin or the languages we spoke made us hypervisible—these markers rendered precarious any presumption of rights within this zone of settler domination. *"The settlers' town is a town of white people, of foreigners."*[25]

CHECKPOINT 300, Bethlehem
11:55. We arrived to Checkpoint 300. Earlier that morning was spent in the Aida Camp where thousands of refugees have lived for decades. From the roof of the community center, I surveyed a landscape of rainwater collection tanks, solar panels, satellite dishes, entangled with phone lines and electrical wires. Our host Abdulfattah Abusour told us that the camp's infrastructures of electricity, water, transport, and communication were all privatized and that water, for example, costs residents in the camp four times what it does elsewhere. The Oslo protocols accorded Israel sole control of importation, exportation, and taxation of most goods and services in the occupied territories.[26] *"The native town is a hungry town, starved of bread, of meat, of shoes, of coal, of light."*[27] I could see the construction of several new units where workers used concrete blocks to partition interior and exterior walls, poured concrete to form floors and columns, and erected concrete switchback stairs to stitch each floor together. *"It is a world without spaciousness; men live there on top of each other, and their huts are built one on top of the other."*[28]

We walked along the border of the Aida Camp where the security barrier enforced the conditions of enclosure hallmark of

Fanon's *"les damnés,"* the wretched, *"it is a town of niggers and dirty Arabs."*[29] The twenty-five-foot wall blocked all movement and obscured views to other parts of Bethlehem. Piles of debris abounded at the base of the wall amid evidence of cycles of destruction and reconstruction. It is *"a town wallowing in the mire."*[30] Scorched carcasses of guard turrets swelled outward from the barrier's ominous verticality. Everywhere in the occupied territories, including here, the barrier had become a canvas for graffiti and murals expressing indignation and outrage at the illegal occupation whose violence had reduced most Palestinians to a condition of bare life. Some of the graffiti memorialized those killed by tear gas and bullets, especially the many children. A small black stencil graffiti on a lower part of the barrier wall depicted a child whose hopscotch game is divided by a coil of barbed wire. This was a chilling reminder that the brutal vise of white supremacy chokes off any future for nonwhite life. *"They are born there, it matters little where or how; they die there, it matters not where, nor how."*[31]

To get to the other side of the separation barrier we eventually arrived to Checkpoint 300, Gilo checkpoint, or Bethlehem checkpoint, erected in 2005 at

fig.5
Protocol screening video in Checkpoint 300, Bethlehem, photo by author, 2019

the same time as the wall. Like the Allenby Crossing, its many names illustrated the contested status of this occupied territory. A large banner festooned above the entrance called the checkpoint the "Rachel Tomb's Crossing" whose "humanitarian entry lane" was an attempt to distract tourists from the ritualistic (high-tech) dehumanization that still transpires in this border zone. Like a few other checkpoints, this one had been overhauled in 2019. Because of its increased infrastructure of surveillance to screen workers, residents, and tourists who daily pass through here (all signs were written in Arabic, Hebrew, and English) this checkpoint is also considered a terminal. We wound through one of three exterior security lanes that ran parallel to the barrier. A corrugated fiberglass lean-to roof attached to the barrier wall covered all three lanes. Metal fencing topped the shoulder-high walls to prevent someone from jumping into another lane. Strategically placed cameras observed our movements. These covert forms of surveillance reduced the physical presence of Israeli military, a means of intimidation and a volatile symbol of occupation.

We entered the checkpoint's interior through a pair of revolving metal gates—a now familiar element from the occupation's catalog of racialized enclosures. Once inside the large, double-height, top-lit hall, whose brightness no doubt facilitated the technologies of surveillance making visible all bodies, I walked up an incline also split into three lanes. At the end of the hall, two monitors blared a video whose soundtrack's

pulsing beats were more apropos a bar than a checkpoint. They delivered directions for entry: scan your permit, look into the camera, remove your sunglasses, remove your hat, proceed one person at a time (fig. 5). These border protocols made each body visible for the collection of biometric data that feeds into a national database accessible to entities like the US Department of Homeland Security.[32] The data accumulates into a digital archive of racial difference according to how it sorts "humanity into full humans, not-quite-humans, and nonhumans."[33] This surveillance of Palestinians demonstrates how high-end scanning technologies racialize bodies. According to my fellow PalFest traveler Simone Browne, this process continues a long history of marking bodies, like the way that branding in the *longue durée* of the transatlantic slave trade and slaveholding "was instituted as a means of population management that rendered whiteness prototypical through its making, marking, and marketing of blackness as visible and a commodity."[34] Making Palestinian difference visible normalizes Israeli sovereignty along with the covert whiteness that underwrites it. *"When you examine at close quarters the colonial context, it is evident that what parcels out the world is to begin with the fact of belonging to or not belonging to a given race, a given species."*[35]

Because most of us were foreigners, we were allowed to enter the humanitarian lanes and moved through the checkpoint in less than twenty minutes. However, if we had

129

arrived earlier in the day, we would have witnessed a very different scene, as thousands of Palestinian workers, mostly men, jammed into the entry lanes and queued for screening. Beginning for some before dawn, these workers pass daily through the checkpoint for jobs on the Israeli side of the separation wall or in other Palestinian cities. Workers can wait up to three hours to advance through the screening process.[36] In "checkpoint time," waiting immobilizes, it is a means of wasting time, wasting life.[37] *"No conciliation is possible, for of the two terms, one is superfluous."*

Not only was Palestinian land necessary for the establishment and expansion of the Israeli nation-state through its settler project of dispossession, but Palestinian labor has been essential for the construction of houses, shopping malls, office buildings, roadways, prisons, and a host of other building types.[38] The designation of guest worker in turn affirms the freedom to work as a right of citizenship for Israelis. Under racial capitalism racialization and proletariatization work together as forms of enclosure that enable the exploitation of bodies. As Sylvia Wynter suggests, "Colonization of the popular masses enclosed them in being proletariat—as the black was enclosed in the being of Negro. This enclosure of both was part of the mechanism by which the bourgeoisie introjects its ruling consciousness into all areas of work, and increasingly of play."[39]

Essential to colonialism's domination, dispossession, and wealth accumulation is how gender and sexuality are controlled to serve various extractive regimes. This and other checkpoints have proven no different. Scholar Lisa Lowe reminds us "how colonized populations were differentially racialized through their proximities to normative ideas of family reproduction that became central to early nineteenth century liberalism" and that continue to define today's racialized distributions of freedom and humanity.[40] The ability of male workers to obtain work permits (primarily in the blue-collar sector) reinforces patriarchal categories of men as the primary source of income for Palestinian families, though a small number of women hold work permits. In their fieldwork at Checkpoint 300 and the surrounding neighborhoods, scholars Mark Griffith and Jemima Repo learned that the opaque process of permit acquisition discourages many women from seeking them for medical, religious, or cultural purposes.[41] If women are successful in securing permits, the experience of the checkpoint can be daunting, even with the addition of the humanitarian lane, which could be shut down at any time, and difficult because of harassment during the screening process.[42] As a consequence, Palestinian women are immobilized by this racializing assemblage of barriers, borders, and checkpoints.

I exited Checkpoint 300 along Hebron Road near a bus stop: infrastructure is the settler's privilege. *"The settler's feet are never visible, except perhaps in the sea; but there you're never close enough to see them."* These buses transport marked bodies—guest workers and noncitizens—to sites of extraction. Enclosures, after all, can be mobile. To wit, the slave ship was a key apparatus of the racial assemblage of the transatlantic slave trade. The ship's dank, cramped hold was the time-space enclosure that dehumanized the African into the Negro, the Black, and the fungible thing, which in turn not only produced profit to construct splendid edifices of the Metropole but also generated the signifiers of whiteness and mastery, history, and geography definitive of modernity and the West. The colonial formation of the hold and its immanent death never disappeared, but haunts the everyday life of marked bodies—like those in occupied Palestine—as theorist Christina Sharpe puts it, "its long wake, the residence time of the hold, its longue durée."[43] While we waited for all to clear the screening process and for our bus to take us to Ramallah, our group gathered on the sidewalk, with some of us sitting on a stone wall. In the distance appeared the red roofs of the housing complexes of the Gilo settlement. Across the street I noticed a beautiful carpet of yellow wildflowers stretching to a large olive grove—trees once owned and tended by Palestinian residents of Bethlehem. This experience of calm and spaciousness after and adjacent to the hurriedness and density of the places we had visited in the morning—Aida Refugee Camp and the barrier—rendered the pictur-esque scene deeply unsettling in *"this world divided into compartments."*[44] ●

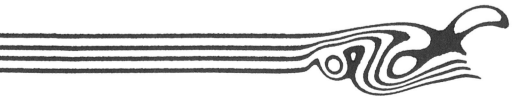

ENDNOTES

1. Frantz Fanon, *The Wretched of the Earth*, trans. Constance Farrington (New York: Grove Press, 1963), 38–39.

2. Helga Tawil-Souri, "Checkpoint Time," *Qui Parle* 26, no. 2 (December 2017): 400.

3. Fanon, *Wretched of the Earth*, 37.

4. See United Nations Office for the Coordination of Humanitarian Affairs (OCHA), "Over 700 Road Obstacles Control Palestinian Movement within the West Bank," October 8, 2018, https://www.ochaopt.org/content/over-700-road-obstacles-control-palestinian-movement-within-west-bank.

5. Scholars and activists have noted the biopolitical dimensions of this process. Michel Foucault sketches out his theory of the biopolitical as a regime of power, biopower, that works in concert with disciplinary power that individuates. Biopower functions at the scale of the population as a "power of regularization, and it, in contrast consists in making live and letting die." See Michel Foucault, "17 March 1976," in *Society Must Be Defended - Lectures at the Collège de France*, trans. David Macey (New York: Picador, 1997), 247.

6. Alexander G. Weheliye, *Habeas Viscus: Racializing Assemblages, Biopolitics, and Black Feminist Theories of the Human* (Durham, NC: Duke University Press, 2014), 3–4.

7. Saidiya Hartman, "The End of White Supremacy, An American Romance," *Bomb Magazine*, June 5, 2020, https://bombmagazine.org/articles/the-end-of-white-supremacy-an-american-romance/.

8. Fanon, *Wretched of the Earth*, 37–38.

9. Eyal Weizman, *Hollow Land: Israel's Architecture of Occupation* (London and New York: Verso Books, 2007), 5.

10. Fanon, *Wretched of the Earth*, 39.

11. Hibo Bou Akar, *For the War Yet to Come, Planning Beirut's Frontiers* (Stanford: Stanford University Press, 2018), 7.

12. Fanon, *Wretched of the Earth*, 38.

13. Fanon, *Wretched of the Earth*, 38.

14. Fanon, *Wretched of the Earth*, 38.

15. Fanon, *Wretched of the Earth*, 38.

16. Fanon, *Wretched of the Earth*, 38.

17. Fanon, *Wretched of the Earth*, 38.

18. "An Evident Extrajudicial Execution in Hebron," *International Solidarity Movement*, March 24, 2016, https://palsolidarity.org/2016/03/an-evident-extrajudicial-execution-in-hebron/.

19. Fanon, *Wretched of the Earth*, 38.

20. "Police (Shoter)/Hebron DCO/Bab a-Zawiya (56)," B'Tselem – The Israeli Information Center for Human Rights in the Occupied Territories,https://www.btselem.org/node/203027

21. Fanon, *Wretched of the Earth*, 38–39.

22. Fanon, *Wretched of the Earth*, 37.

23. Fanon, *Wretched of the Earth*, 38.

24. Fanon, *Wretched of the Earth*, 37.

25. Fanon, *Wretched of the Earth*, 38.

26. Andrew Ross, *Stonemen: The Palestinians Who Built Israel* (London and New York: Verso Books, 2021), 127.

27. Fanon, *Wretched of the Earth*, 38.

28. Fanon, *Wretched of the Earth*, 38.

29. Fanon, *Wretched of the Earth*, 38.

30. Fanon, *Wretched of the Earth*, 38.

31. Fanon, *Wretched of the Earth*, 38.

32. US Department of Homeland Security, "DHS to Increase Security Cooperation with Israel through New Arrangements," DHS press release, March 3, 2022, https://www.dhs.gov/news/2022/03/03/dhs-increase-security-cooperation-israel-through-new-arrangements.

33. Weheliye, *Habeas Viscus*, 4.

34. Simone Browne, *Dark Matters: On the Surveillance of Blackness* (Durham, NC: Duke University Press, 2015), 118.

35. Fanon, *Wretched of the Earth*, 38–39.

36. Jaclyn Ashly, "Israel's Checkpoint 300: Suffocation and Broken Ribs at Rush Hour," *Al Jazeera*, March 13, 2019, https://www.aljazeera.com/features/2019/3/13/israels-checkpoint-300-suffocation-and-broken-ribs-at-rush-hour.

37. Tawil-Souri, "Checkpoint Time," 400.

38. See Ross, *Stonemen*, 22–23. An estimated 133,000 Palestinians worked in Israel in 2019. See International Labor Organization (ILO), "The Situation of Workers of the Occupied Arab Territories," International Labor Conference, 109th session, 2021, online report, 6, https://www.ilo.org/wcmsp5/groups/public/---ed_norm/---relconf/documents/meetingdocument/wcms_745966.pdf.

39. Sylvia Wynter, "Black Metamorphosis" (unpublished manuscript, 1970s).

40. Lisa Lowe, *The Intimacies of the Four Continents* (Durham, NC: Duke University Press, 2015), 36.

41. Mark Griffiths and Jemima Repo, "Women and Checkpoints in Palestine," *Security Dialogue* 52, no. 3 (2021): 253–54. For further reading on spatial politics of Checkpoint 300, see Mark Griffiths and Jemima Repo, "Biopolitics and Checkpoint 300 in Occupied Palestine: Bodies, Affect, Discipline," *Political Geography* no. 65 (2018) and Alexandra Rijke and Claudio Minca, "Inside Checkpoint 300: Checkpoint Regimes as Spatial Political Technologies in the Occupied Palestinian Territories," *Antipode* 51, no. 3 (2019).

42. Griffiths and Repo, "Women and Checkpoints," 256.

43. Christina Sharpe, *In the Wake: On Blackness and Being* (Durham, NC: Duke University Press, 2016), 70.

44. Fanon, *Wretched of the Earth*, 38.

ACKNOWLEDGMENTS

This anthology is a collective endeavor and would not have been possible otherwise. I have learned tremendously from each and every person listed here. I would first like to thank Yasmin El-Rifae for her careful eyes and brilliant mind in her copyediting efforts, Omar Robert Hamilton for ongoing support and solidarity in this volume and beyond, and the PalFest team of interlocutors, including Jehan Bseiso, Maath Musleh, Sharif Abdel Kouddous, and John Horner.

I am infinitely thankful to Natalie Diaz and the Center for Imagination in the Borderlands (CIB) at Arizona State University for their support here and beyond. This volume is in part made possible thanks to the Matakyev Research Fellowship at CIB. I would like to thank Tala Safié and Bráulio Amado for tirelessly employing their genius of design to interpret and prop up the writings in this volume. I would like to thank the authors, scholars, and thinkers who participated in the PalFest 2019 festival *Urban Futures: Colonial Space Today* and everyone who hosted us in Jerusalem, Ramallah, Bethlehem, Hebron, Lydd, and Haifa. The 2019 festival acted as a powerful catalyst for multiple collaborative projects, including this very volume. I would also like to thank Ian Edward Wallace for endless nights of editorial and moral support; Alessandra Amin and Nadine Fattaleh for helping me workshop the introductory text in the most brilliant of ways. I would also like to acknowledge the following people and places for generously providing me with spaces to write and edit, between 2021 and 2023, including but not limited to: the Educational Bookshop in Jerusalem, Haifa and Youssef Sabbagh, Dung Ngo, and the Brooklyn Public Library. Finally, I would like to thank the Haymarket team, especially Anthony Arnove, Maria Isabelle Carlos, Rachel Cohen, and Eric Kerl.

INDEX

CONTRIBUTOR BIOGRAPHIES

BRÁULIO AMADO is a Portuguese graphic designer and illustrator currently living in New York City. He makes posters, record covers, editorial illustrations, videos, and some other stuff.

TAREQ BACONI is a writer. He is the author of *Hamas Contained: The Rise and Pacification of Palestinian Resistance* (Stanford University Press, 2018). Tareq's writing has appeared in the *London Review of Books*, the *New York Review of Books*, the *Baffler*, the *Nation*, *Skin Deep*, and the *Washington Post*, among others. He serves as the president of the board of Al-Shabaka: The Palestinian Policy Network, the book review editor for the *Journal of Palestine Studies*, and cofounder of Makan. Tareq is the former senior analyst for Israel/Palestine and Economics of Conflict at the International Crisis Group, based in Ramallah. He is currently completing a manuscript about queer love in Amman.

JEHAN BSEISO is a Palestinian poet, researcher, and aid worker. Her poetry has been published in several online and offline platforms.

Her coauthored book, *I Remember My Name*, is the Palestine Book Awards winner in the creative category (2016). She is the coeditor of *Making Mirrors: Writing/Righting by and for Refugees* (2019) and is on the production team of the Palestine Festival of Literature. Bseiso has been working with Médecins sans Frontières/Doctors Without Borders (MSF) since 2008 and is currently the deputy general director of the Operational Center in Brussels.

KELLER EASTERLING is a writer, designer, and the Enid Storm Dwyer Professor of Architecture at Yale. Her books include *Medium Design* (Verso, 2021), *Extrastatecraft: The Power of Infrastructure Space* (Verso, 2014), *Subtraction* (Sternberg, 2014), *Enduring Innocence: Global Architecture and its Political Masquerades* (MIT, 2005), and *Organization Space: Landscapes, Highways and Houses in America* (MIT, 1999). Easterling is also the coauthor (with Richard Prelinger) of *Call it Home*, a laserdisc/DVD history of US suburbia from 1934 to 1960. Easterling lectures, publishes, and exhibits internationally.

Her research and writing was included in the 2014 and 2018 Venice Biennales. Easterling is a 2019 United States Artist in Architecture and Design.

OMAR ROBERT HAMILTON is a writer and filmmaker working between Europe and the Arab World. His first novel, *The City Always Wins* (Faber & Faber, 2017), won the Society of Authors' Best Debut Under 35. He most recently coedited *You Have Not Yet Been Defeated* (Fitzcarraldo Editions, 2021), the selected works of the imprisoned writer, Alaa Abd el-Fattah. He is the director of the Palestine Festival of Literature.

SAMIA HENNI is a historian of the built, destroyed, and imagined environments. She is the author of the multi-award-winning *Architecture of Counterrevolution: The French Army in Northern Algeria* (gta Verlag 2017, EN; Editions B42, 2019, FR), the editor of *Deserts Are Not Empty* (Columbia Books on Architecture and the City, 2022) and *War Zones* (gta Verlag, 2018). She is also the maker of exhibitions, such as *Archives: Secret-Défense?* (ifa Gallery,

SAVVY Contemporary, Berlin, 2021), *Housing Pharmacology* (Manifesta 13, Marseille, 2020), *and Discreet Violence: Architecture and the French War in Algeria* (Zurich, Rotterdam, Berlin, Johannesburg, Paris, Prague, Ithaca, Philadelphia, Charlottesville, 2017–22). She was Albert Hirschman Chair (2020–21) at the Institute of Advanced Study in Marseille and a Geddes Fellow (2021) at Edinburgh School of Architecture and Landscape Architecture. Henni received her PhD in the history and theory of architecture (with distinction, ETH Medal) from ETH Zurich and taught at Princeton University, ETH Zurich, the University of Zurich, and the Geneva University of Art and Design. Currently, she is working on an exhibition and a book project on France's nuclear infrastructure and wastes in the Sahara. Henni teaches at the Department of Architecture, Cornell University's College of Architecture, Art, and Planning.

ELLEN VAN NEERVEN is a writer of Mununjali and Dutch heritage. They are the author of a collection of stories, *Heat and Light* (2014), plus two poetry collections, *Comfort Food* (2016) and *Throat* (2020), all published by University of Queensland Press. They live and work on the unceded lands of the Turrbal and Yagera peoples.

DINA OMAR is a doctoral candidate in anthropology at Yale University with a joint certification in Women, Gender, and Sexuality Studies. Omar is an academic, activist, writer, and entrepreneur. Her most recent venture is as the owner of the Palestinian Soap Cooperative. She studied and taught with June Jordan's Poetry for the People program at UC Berkeley between 2006 and 2010. Her dissertation examines the politics of mental health under conditions of extreme surveillance in the context of the United States, Israel, and Palestine.

KAREEM RABIE is assistant professor of anthropology at the University of Illinois at Chicago and the author of *Palestine Is Throwing a Party and the Whole World Is Invited: Capital and State Building in the West Bank*, published in 2021 with Duke University Press.

YASMIN EL-RIFAE is a writer and editor in Cairo and London. She works with *Mada Masr* in Cairo and is a coproducer of the Palestine Festival of Literature. She is the author of *Radius: A Story of Feminist Revolution* (Verso, 2022). Her writing has appeared in the *Guardian*, the *Nation*, *Lux*, *LitHub*, and *Guernica*.

MAHDI SABBAGH is a writer and urbanist. He is a co-curator of the Palestine Festival of Literature and Editor at large at the Avery Review. His work has been published in the *Journal of Public Culture*, *Jerusalem Quarterly*, *Architecture of the Territory* (Kaph Books, 2022), *Open Gaza* (AUC Press, 2021), *Awham Magazine*, *Curbed*, *the Funambulist*, and *Arab Urbanism*. Mahdi is a 2023 Matakyev Research Fellow at the Center for Imagination in the Borderlands.

TALA SAFIÉ is a graphic designer and art director from Beirut based in New York.

OMER SHAH is a cultural anthropologist. He is the Chau Mellon Postdoctoral Fellow in the department of anthropology at Pomona College. He received his doctorate in anthropology from Columbia University in 2021. His dissertation project is titled, "Made in Mecca: Expertise, Smart Technology, and Hospitality in the Post-Oil Holy City." In it, he examines an emerging world of crowd scientists, engineers, and other "hajj entrepreneurs" and "experts" making new smart technologies of mass pilgrim management, logistics, and surveillance. His research has been supported by grants from both the Social Science Research Council and the Wenner Gren Foundation.

Cultural historian, architectural designer, and curator MABEL O. WILSON teaches architecture and Black studies at Columbia University, where she also serves as the director of the Institute for Research in African American Studies. With her practice Studio&, she was a member of the design team that recently completed the Memorial to Enslaved Laborers at the University of Virginia. Wilson has authored *Begin with the Past: Building the National Museum of African American* *History and Culture* (2016) and *Negro Building: Black Americans in the World of Fairs and Museums* (2012) and coedited the volume *Race and Modern Architecture: From the Enlightenment to Today* (2020). She is a founding member of Who Builds Your Architecture? (WBYA?), an advocacy project to educate the architectural profession about the problems of globalization and labor. For the Museum of Modern Art in New York City, she was cocurator of the exhibition *Reconstructions: Architecture and Blackness in America* (2021).

Milton Keynes UK
Ingram Content Group UK Ltd.
UKHW050238110624
443876UK00003B/23